Bridge for the Connoisseur

A new book by Hugh Kelsey is always a welcome event, and this one will have special appeal for those who appreciate the finer points of the game. The 58 deals have been chosen for their artistic value and you will find moments of stark beauty mingled with instructive points in bidding, play and defence. Many of the hands come from international tournaments and relate the brilliancies and the blunders of the stars.

Hugh Kelsey has a world-wide reputation for accurate analysis and lucid prose, and these qualities combine to make this book a rewarding read.

by HUGH KELSEY in the *Master Bridge Series*

TRIPLE SQUEEZES

DOUBLE SQUEEZES

STRIP-SQUEEZES

SIMPLE SQUEEZES

IMPROVE YOUR PARTNER'S DEFENCE

SHARPEN YOUR BRIDGE TECHNIQUE

WINNING CARD PLAY

SLAM BIDDING

LOGICAL BRIDGE PLAY

TEST YOUR CARD PLAY—1

TEST YOUR CARD PLAY—2

TEST YOUR DEFENSIVE PLAY

TEST YOUR PAIRS PLAY

TEST YOUR FINESSING

TEST YOUR TRUMP CONTROL

TEST YOUR COMMUNICATIONS

TEST YOUR CARD-READING

TEST YOUR TIMING

TEST YOUR PERCENTAGES

TEST YOUR ELIMINATION PLAY

TEST YOUR SAFETY PLAY

INSTANT GUIDE TO BRIDGE

START BRIDGE THE EASY WAY

MASTER SQUEEZE PLAY

MASTER PERCENTAGES IN BRIDGE

MASTER FINESSING

MASTER SLAM BIDDING

MASTER SIGNALS

MASTER DOUBLES (with Ron Klinger)

ADVENTURES IN CARD PLAY (with Géza Ottlik)

BRIDGE ODDS FOR PRACTICAL PLAYERS (with Michael Glauert)

IMPROVE YOUR OPENING LEADS (with John Matheson)

Bridge for the Connoisseur

HUGH KELSEY

LONDON
VICTOR GOLLANCZ LTD
in association with
PETER CRAWLEY
1991

First published in Great Britain 1991
in association with Peter Crawley
by Victor Gollancz Ltd,
14 Henrietta Street, London WC2E 8QJ

British Library Cataloguing in Publication Data
Kelsey, H. W. (Hugh Walter)
  Bridge for the connoisseur.—(Master bridge series).
  1. Contract bridge
  I. Title II. Series
  795.415

ISBN 0-575-04996-0

Photoset in Great Britain by
Rowland Phototypesetting Ltd, Bury St Edmunds, Suffolk
and printed in Great Britain by St Edmundsbury Press Ltd,
Bury St Edmunds, Suffolk

Contents

	Introduction	9
1	Worthy of Gold	11
2	Pressure Play	14
3	Missed Chances	16
4	A Matter of Timing	18
5	Ducks in Season	20
6	A Small Tragedy	22
7	Basic Error	24
8	No Second Chance	26
9	Profit without Honour	28
10	Move and Countermove	30
11	The Better Way	32
12	Secrets Revealed	34
13	Uncertain Outcome	36
14	Elegant Unblock	38
15	Comedy Show	40
16	Illusion	42
17	The Lesser Risk	44
18	Test for Both Sides	46
19	No Justice	48
20	Unexpected Thrust	50
21	A Gruesome Slam	52
22	Finely Balanced	54
23	No Trumpets	56
24	Cold Game	58
25	Care Required	61
26	Brilliant Enough	63
27	Amusing for Some	66
28	On the Screen	68
29	Bricks Without Straw	70
30	The Right Choice	72
31	Firework Display	74
32	Too Strong	78
33	Cut and Run	80
34	Theory and Practice	82
35	Animal Farm	84

36	The Hard Way	86
37	Up to a Point	89
38	Innocent Fun	92
39	Midnight Oil	94
40	Exit Card	96
41	Unlikely Spot	98
42	Means of Access	100
43	A Chance from Nowhere	102
44	Option Retained	104
45	Second Suit	106
46	Never Say Die	109
47	Trial and Error	112
48	One Good Card	116
49	Not Perfect	118
50	Going for Eleven	121
51	Never Mind the Jargon	123
52	Table Presents	125
53	Tricky all Round	127
54	A Dummy Squeeze	129
55	Many Ways Home	131
56	A Wasted Asset	134
57	Troubled Waters	137
58	Glimmer of Light	140

Introduction

Our game is still surrounded by a wall of ignorance. I had long suspected that many people glanced at my newspaper columns without actually reading them, and confirmation arrived one day in the form of a letter from a staff journalist on my own paper. He had been charged with co-ordinating the launch of a quarterly 'construction review' and invited my help in the listing of new projects, asking about contractors, specifications, completion dates and so on. I had to explain to the poor fellow that my contracts were different from his and that my knowledge of the stresses on beams and girders could be written on the back of a postage stamp.

A similar experience came my way some years ago when I embarked on a North Cape cruise from South Queensferry, near Edinburgh. 'I'm the bridge expert,' I announced at the top of the gangway and was surprised to be accorded v.i.p. treatment. It was assumed that my task was to pilot the 'Vistafjord' between the daunting pillars of the Forth road and rail bridges.

Fortunately there are a few people in the world who know what bridge is all about and who appreciate the finer points of the game. The hands in this book have been selected for their artistic value and they contain instructive points in play and defence. If you also find them entertaining I shall be well pleased.

1   *Worthy of Gold*

In the women's final of the 1988 Olympiad Denmark made history by defeating Great Britain to become champions. This hand shows the Danish women earning their gold medals.

```
                    ♠ 6 5
                    ♡ A 9 8 7 3 2
                    ◇ K 9 3
                    ♣ J 7
    ♠ K J 9 8 7                    ♠ 10 4 3
    ♡ J 6          N               ♡ K Q 10 5
    ◇ Q 8 7 6 5 4  W    E          ◇ 2
    ♣ —               S            ♣ Q 8 6 4 3
                    ♠ A Q 2
                    ♡ 4
N–S game            ◇ A J 10
Dealer East         ♣ A K 10 9 5 2
```

West	North	East	South
Norris	Brunner	Schaltz	Landy
		Pass	1♣
3♣	3♡	3♠	3NT
4♠	Pass	Pass	4NT
Pass	Pass	Dble	Pass
Pass	Pass		

The jump cue-bid of three clubs was 'Copenhagen', showing spades and diamonds, and West persevered with four spades over three no-trumps. Either North or South might have doubled this, but the double would have brought in no more than 300. Reluctant to give up her vulnerable game, Landy pressed on with four no-trumps, a contract that would have been made with an overtrick on a spade or a diamond lead. But Dorthe Schaltz doubled to indicate strength in hearts and her partner duly led the jack of hearts, presenting South with a formidable problem.

After some reflection Landy adopted the simple line of winning immediately with the ace of hearts and running the jack of clubs. If West had a singleton heart, she would be able to survive a losing club finesse. What she could not survive was the 5-0 club split. There were only nine tricks to be taken, and Denmark gained 13 i.m.p. when South was allowed to play in three no-trumps in the other room.

It is interesting to speculate on what might have happened if Landy had played low at trick one. No doubt East would overtake with the heart queen and return the ten of spades. South might play low at trick two and insert the spade queen at trick three, hoping for a squeeze against East in hearts and clubs. If West continues with a third round of spades this squeeze duly materialises. Declarer wins with the ace of spades and plays the diamond ace followed by the jack. West makes a nuisance of herself by covering with the queen of diamonds to leave the position shown in the diagram.

```
                 ♠ —
                 ♡ A 9 8 7
                 ♢ 9
                 ♣ J 7
    ♠ 9 8                    ♠ —
    ♡ 6            N         ♡ K 10
    ♢ 8 7 6 5   W   E        ♢ —
    ♣ —            S         ♣ Q 8 6 4 3
                 ♠ —
                 ♡ —
                 ♢ 10
                 ♣ A K 10 9 5 2
```

Declarer cashes the ace of hearts, discarding the blocking ten of diamonds from hand, and the play of the nine of diamonds puts the screw on East.

All very pretty, but the defenders can prevail if West switches back to hearts when in with the king of spades. This forces declarer to take the ace of hearts prematurely, preventing the unblock of the diamonds and denying declarer a squeeze card in dummy.

The winning line of play for declarer is to go up with the ace of spades in the second round of the suit. After the play of the ace of diamonds and the jack of diamonds covered by the queen and king, this is the position.

South unblocks the ten of diamonds on the heart ace and plays the nine of diamonds, forcing East to part with her spade. A heart is then conceded, and East has to yield the rest of the tricks on her club return.

But this is double-dummy stuff. The swing on the board was generated not by the declarer's failure to find an exotic line of play but by the bold Danish bidding and the inspired double of four no-trumps.

```
                    ♠ —
                    ♡ A 9 8 7 3
                    ♢ 9
                    ♣ J 7
   ♠ K J 9                        ♠ 3
   ♡ 6          N                 ♡ K 10
   ♢ 8 7 6 5  W   E               ♢ —
   ♣ —            S               ♣ Q 8 6 4 3
                    ♠ Q
                    ♡ —
                    ♢ 10
                    ♣ A K 10 9 5 2
```

The Danish women did not have things all their own way in the final of the 1988 Olympiad. On this hand the swing went to Great Britain.

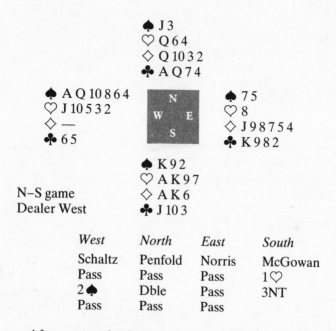

♠ J 3
♥ Q 6 4
♦ Q 10 3 2
♣ A Q 7 4

♠ A Q 10 8 6 4   ♠ 7 5
♥ J 10 5 3 2   ♥ 8
♦ —   ♦ J 9 8 7 5 4
♣ 6 5   ♣ K 9 8 2

♠ K 9 2
♥ A K 9 7
♦ A K 6
♣ J 10 3

N–S game
Dealer West

West	North	East	South
Schaltz	Penfold	Norris	McGowan
Pass	Pass	Pass	1♡
2♠	Dble	Pass	3NT
Pass	Pass	Pass	

After an opening heart bid, a weak jump overcall from West and a negative double from North, South closed the auction with a jump to three no-trumps.

The opening lead of the eight of spades was won by the jack and a diamond was played to the ace. When West threw a heart Liz McGowan had food for thought. Since West had not opened with a 'multi' two diamonds, it seemed quite likely that she would have a secondary heart suit. West discarded a club on the king of diamonds and a spade when a third diamond was played to dummy's queen. A heart to the ace brought the eight from East, and West covered the nine of hearts on the next round.

When East showed out the hand was an open book. After cashing the ace of clubs, declarer was in the happy position of being able to end-play West in either major. In practice she played a spade to the nine and ten, collecting two further heart tricks at the end.

In the other room Bettina Kalkerup played in three no-trumps after an overcall of one spade by West. The opening lead was the same, and declarer again started with the ace and king of diamonds. Pat Davies in the West seat kept her clubs, discarding a heart and a spade, and she threw a further spade when a third diamond was played to the queen. Now there was no way for South to make more than eight tricks and Britain gained 12 i.m.p.

Should declarer have done better? It was not so easy to read the position in this room, but if declarer had taken the view that West, who passed originally, was not likely to have the king of clubs she might still have made her contract. That third round of diamonds is a mistake when West keeps two clubs. As soon as a spade has been discarded, all declarer need do is exit in spades. If West takes her four spade tricks, clubs are thrown from dummy and a heart and a club from hand, and East is squeezed in the minors on the run of the hearts. If West refuses to cash all her spades, South can establish her ninth trick in clubs.

3   *Missed Chances*

Bridge is difficult because players have to take action on the basis of incomplete information, which means that chances are often missed by both sides in the early stages. This hand from a round-robin match in the 1985 Bermuda Bowl struck me as amusing.

♠ J 10 7 5 2
♡ K Q 3
◇ J 10
♣ 9 5 4

♠ 6 3
♡ A 8 7 2
◇ 8 5 3
♣ A Q 6 3

♠ K 8
♡ J
◇ Q 9 7 4
♣ K J 10 8 7 2

♠ A Q 9 4
♡ 10 9 6 5 4
◇ A K 6 2
♣ —

Game all
Dealer South

South	West	North	East
1♡	Pass	1♠	2♣
4♣	Dble	Pass	5♣
Pass	Pass	5♡	Pass
Pass	Pass		

Four of a major was the contract at all the other tables, but in the match between Israel and New Zealand the Israelis allowed themselves to be pushed to the five-level.

The declarer ruffed the club lead and played a heart to the king, eyeing East's jack with suspicion. After a successful spade finesse he played a second trump, winning with the queen when West again played low. A third round of trumps would clearly have been fatal, so South played on spades. West ruffed the third spade, cashed the ace of hearts and exited with a club, forcing out

16

declarer's last trump. Two more spades were won in dummy and the jack of diamonds was led in the diagram position:

East naturally covered with the queen of diamonds, and South had to lose a diamond or a club at the end.

The ending was foreseeable and South could have done better. When in dummy with the second heart he should take the diamond finesse. At this stage it makes no difference whether East covers or not. South scores three diamonds and reverts to spades, and if West refuses to ruff the third spade South ruffs his fourth diamond in dummy. All the defenders can make are two trumps.

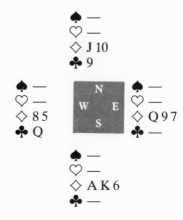

♠ —
♡ —
♢ J 10
♣ 9

♠ —
♡ —
♢ 8 5
♣ Q

♠ —
♡ —
♢ Q 9 7
♣ —

♠ —
♡ —
♢ A K 6
♣ —

South need not have been given this chance, however. If West plays the ace of hearts on the second round and continues clubs, declarer has no way of making more than ten tricks.

North might have saved the day by bidding five spades instead of five hearts, for his partner's splinter bid of four clubs had promised spade support. Five spades is a viable contract. If the defenders start with a heart to the ace and a heart ruff, they make no further tricks. If they start with clubs, declarer enters hand with a third-round diamond ruff, draws trumps and plays on hearts. He can actually make twelve tricks if he unblocks the king or queen of hearts under the ace.

But the best solution for North is to double five clubs. This contract goes three down for a penalty of 800.

In the round robin of the 1985 Venice Cup the British women had trouble with their opponents from Chinese Taipei, who bid every slam in sight and got away with murder on a couple of occasions. Here is an example.

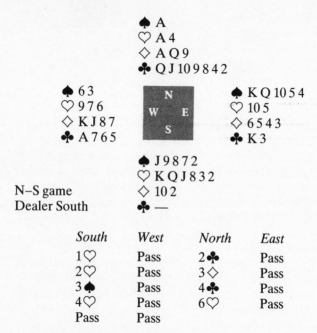

```
                    ♠ A
                    ♡ A 4
                    ◇ A Q 9
                    ♣ Q J 10 9 8 4 2

        ♠ 6 3          N          ♠ K Q 10 5 4
        ♡ 9 7 6     W     E       ♡ 10 5
        ◇ K J 8 7               ◇ 6 5 4 3
        ♣ A 7 6 5      S          ♣ K 3

                    ♠ J 9 8 7 2
                    ♡ K Q J 8 3 2
   N–S game          ◇ 10 2
   Dealer South      ♣ —
```

South	West	North	East
1♡	Pass	2♣	Pass
2♡	Pass	3◇	Pass
3♠	Pass	4♣	Pass
4♡	Pass	6♡	Pass
Pass	Pass		

Aggressive Chinese bidding led to an optimistic slam which would have had little chance on a spade lead. West decided to lead the jack of diamonds, however. No doubt it seemed a good idea at the time. The declarer won with the queen, unblocking the ten from her hand. The slam could have been made in comfort by establishing the clubs, but South elected to go for a cross-ruff instead. She cashed the spade ace, ruffed a club, finessed the nine of diamonds, cashed the diamond ace for a spade discard, and ruffed another club. A spade ruff was followed by another club from dummy, but East ruffed with the ten of hearts and declarer had to over-ruff with the jack. This left the position shown in the diagram.

When a spade was led West erred by throwing the king of diamonds. After ruffing with the ace of hearts, declarer was able to ruff another club with the heart eight and claim twelve tricks.

It is a different story if West discards the ace of clubs when a spade is led in the diagram position. East ruffs the next club with the five of hearts and the defenders score two tricks. (Note that if South over-ruffs with the queen of hearts, West has to under-ruff.)

Better timing of the cross-ruff would have given the defenders no chance. After cashing the ace of spades and ruffing a club, declarer should ruff a spade, ruff another club, and ruff a spade with the heart ace. A third club is ruffed with the heart ten and over-ruffed with the jack, but declarer is in a position to draw East's last trump before finessing the diamond nine and cashing the ace.

Now it makes no difference if West has kept the diamond king instead of the club ace. South discards her remaining spade on a club and West has to concede the last two tricks.

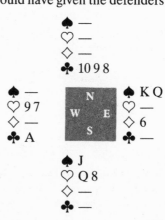

5 Ducks in Season

Defenders who take their aces and kings at the first opportunity make life far too easy for the declarer. It is usually right to conserve high cards even when a singleton is led from dummy. An amusing example of this type of defence came up in the match between Paraguay and Venezuela in the 1984 Olympiad.

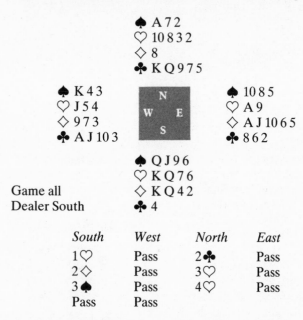

```
                         ♠ A 7 2
                         ♡ 10 8 3 2
                         ◇ 8
                         ♣ K Q 9 7 5
         ♠ K 4 3                              ♠ 10 8 5
         ♡ J 5 4              N               ♡ A 9
         ◇ 9 7 3          W       E           ◇ A J 10 6 5
         ♣ A J 10 3           S               ♣ 8 6 2
                         ♠ Q J 9 6
                         ♡ K Q 7 6
Game all                 ◇ K Q 4 2
Dealer South             ♣ 4
```

South	West	North	East
1♡	Pass	2♣	Pass
2◇	Pass	3♡	Pass
3♠	Pass	4♡	Pass
Pass	Pass		

The Paraguayans pressed hard in the bidding to reach a close game. The defenders have three aces to cash, but they are all well placed for the declarer. The spade finesse is also right, and it looks as though the contract should be made in comfort. But the Venezuelan defenders were the veterans Roberto Benaim and Francis Vernon and they had different ideas.

Benaim led the four of hearts to his partner's ace and the heart continuation was won by the king. Declarer led the four of clubs at trick three and, although this was clearly a singleton, Benaim did the right thing by playing low (duck number one). The queen of clubs won the trick and the eight of diamonds was returned. Now it was East's turn to play low (duck number two). South won with the queen and advanced the queen of spades on which West played low (duck number three). All these ducks were necessary to give the defenders any chance at all. If either minor ace had been taken on the first round, or if the queen of spades had been covered, the declarer could hardly have gone wrong. At this point the position was as shown in the diagram.

Bemused by the reluctance of his opponents to take their tricks, the declarer embarked on a cross-ruff, taking two diamond ruffs in dummy and two club ruffs in hand. Neither of the missing aces made an appearance, however, and South was held to nine tricks —five trumps, two spades, and trick in each of the minor suits.

In spite of the sharp defence the contract could have been

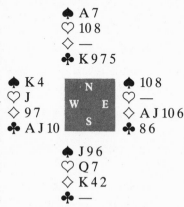

♠ A 7
♡ 10 8
◇ —
♣ K 9 7 5

♠ K 4   ♠ 10 8
♡ J   ♡ —
◇ 9 7   ◇ A J 10 6
♣ A J 10   ♣ 8 6

♠ J 9 6
♡ Q 7
◇ K 4 2
♣ —

made. Do you see how? In the diagram position South should draw the last trump and continue with the ace and another spade. This gains an extra spade trick in exchange for one of his trump tricks and at the same time enforces an end-play. In with the king of spades, West has to yield the tenth trick in either clubs or diamonds.

6 *A Small Tragedy*

Defenders sometimes have difficulty in cashing the tricks that are rightfully theirs against a contract of three no-trumps. Here is an example from a pairs game.

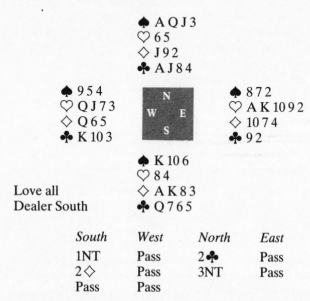

```
                    ♠ A Q J 3
                    ♡ 6 5
                    ◇ J 9 2
                    ♣ A J 8 4
    ♠ 9 5 4                        ♠ 8 7 2
    ♡ Q J 7 3          N           ♡ A K 10 9 2
    ◇ Q 6 5        W       E       ◇ 10 7 4
    ♣ K 10 3           S           ♣ 9 2
                    ♠ K 10 6
                    ♡ 8 4
Love all            ◇ A K 8 3
Dealer South        ♣ Q 7 6 5
```

South	West	North	East
1NT	Pass	2♣	Pass
2◇	Pass	3NT	Pass
Pass	Pass		

Four spades is unquestionably a better spot but, after a weak no-trump and a Stayman enquiry, South found himself at the wheel in three no-trumps.

West led the three of hearts, which looked like a good start for the defence. East won with the king and continued with the ace of hearts on which West played the seven. Now there was no way for the defenders to cash their fifth heart trick. You might think this should make no difference, since declarer appears to have no more than eight tricks anyway. But in such situations the ninth trick is never far away.

The defenders continued with two more rounds of hearts, declarer discarding two clubs from dummy and a diamond and a club from his hand. West switched to a spade and South, who had resigned himself to one down, shot up in his chair and took notice. Winning the spade in hand, he finessed the club jack successfully, played a diamond to his king, and continued with spades to reach the position shown in the diagram.

South discarded the eight of diamonds on the spade ace, and the goddess of blockages, who had frowned on the defenders, produced a smile for declarer when West was caught in a criss-cross squeeze.

If West had thrown a club, South would have cashed the club ace and made the rest of the tricks in his hand. When in

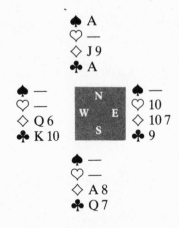

practice West threw a diamond, South played a diamond to his ace and crossed back in clubs to enjoy the established jack of diamonds.

How should this defensive tragedy have been avoided? West might have started with the queen of hearts, it is true, but this is not always the best lead from such a holding. Alternatively East might have returned a low heart at trick two, although he would have looked foolish if South had held the doubleton queen. The real solution is for West to unblock one of his heart honours under the ace on the second round of the suit. No risk attaches to this play. Declarer is known to have started with fewer than four hearts in view of his negative response to the Stayman enquiry. East is marked with at least four hearts, and West should start to unblock just in case he has five.

7   Basic Error

The standard counter to aggressive bidding is tight defence, but as long as the latter remains a rare commodity it will play to bid aggressively. Look at what happened on this hand from a multiple teams.

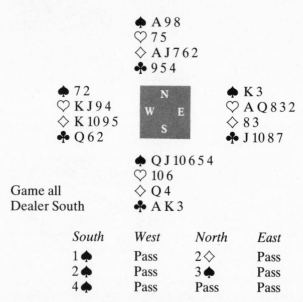

```
                    ♠ A 9 8
                    ♡ 7 5
                    ◇ A J 7 6 2
                    ♣ 9 5 4
    ♠ 7 2                         ♠ K 3
    ♡ K J 9 4          N          ♡ A Q 8 3 2
    ◇ K 10 9 5     W     E        ◇ 8 3
    ♣ Q 6 2           S           ♣ J 10 8 7
                    ♠ Q J 10 6 5 4
                    ♡ 10 6
Game all            ◇ Q 4
Dealer South        ♣ A K 3
```

South	West	North	East
1♠	Pass	2◇	Pass
2♠	Pass	3♠	Pass
4♠	Pass	Pass	Pass

Most of the North–South competitors were content to play in a part-score, but at one table the aggressive spade game was reached. A heart lead went to the ace and the heart return was won by the jack. West switched to the two of clubs and the seven forced out declarer's ace. The spade queen was led for a losing finesse, and East continued hopefully with the jack of clubs.

This defence was not good enough. Declarer won with the king of clubs, played the queen of diamonds to the king and ace, cashed the jack of diamonds and ruffed a third diamond in hand. A trump put dummy in for a further diamond ruff, and the club loser eventually went away on the established long diamond.

East's decision to continue clubs at trick five may look natural enough, but in fact it was a basic error. Although the defenders have to look to clubs for the setting trick, there is no immediate need to knock out the club king. The first priority must be to counter the menace of dummy's long diamond suit, and to this end East should return his second trump. Now declarer lacks the entries to set up an extra diamond trick and the contract drifts one down.

Naturally, South should not have given East this chance to defeat the contract. Needing one of the finesses to be right, he should take the diamond finesse at trick four. When this works he can continue with diamonds, ruffing the third round in hand before trying the spade finesse. East may win and return what he likes, but South cannot be prevented from establishing the long diamond.

This does not mean that the contract should always be made. West might have recognised the threat posed by the diamond suit at an earlier stage. If he switches to a trump at trick three, declarer can never make more than nine tricks.

8   *No Second Chance*

Opportunity seldom knocks twice for the defenders. Here is an instructive slam hand from a team game.

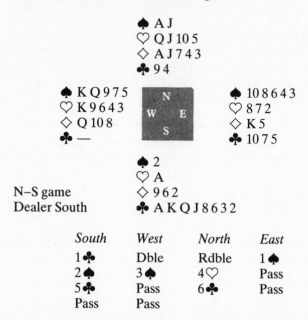

```
                    ♠ A J
                    ♡ Q J 10 5
                    ◇ A J 7 4 3
                    ♣ 9 4
  ♠ K Q 9 7 5          N          ♠ 10 8 6 4 3
  ♡ K 9 6 4 3      W       E      ♡ 8 7 2
  ◇ Q 10 8             S          ◇ K 5
  ♣ —                             ♣ 10 7 5
                    ♠ 2
                    ♡ A
N–S game            ◇ 9 6 2
Dealer South        ♣ A K Q J 8 6 3 2
```

South	West	North	East
1♣	Dble	Rdble	1♠
2♠	3♠	4♡	Pass
5♣	Pass	6♣	Pass
Pass	Pass		

The bidding became a little confused in the middle stages, but South clarified matters with his bid of five clubs and North felt he had enough to raise to six.

The slam was not an unreasonable one, but the automatic lead of the king of spades took out one of dummy's entries and the declarer could not count on scoring a twelfth trick in hearts. South drew the outstanding trumps and played a couple of extra rounds to reach the position shown in the diagram.

Expecting West to have both the king and the queen of diamonds for his takeout double, South played a diamond to dummy's jack, wincing when East produced the king. At this point East could, and should, have defeated the slam by returning his second diamond. Blind to the danger, however, he returned a spade, and there was no second chance for the defence. South ruffed, cashed the ace of hearts, and continued with trumps to squeeze West in the red suits and land his slam.

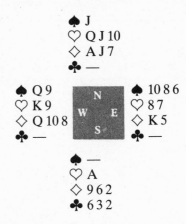

♠ J
♡ Q J 10
♢ A J 7
♣ —

♠ Q 9
♡ K 9
♢ Q 10 8
♣ —

♠ 10 8 6
♡ 8 7
♢ K 5
♣ —

♠ —
♡ A
♢ 9 6 2
♣ 6 3 2

Declarer need not have given East the chance to defeat him, of course. The slam was cold on the assumption that West held length in diamonds along with the major-suit honours. South's mistake lay in giving up the lead too early. If he had cashed the ace of hearts and continued trumps he could have reached the position shown in the second diagram.

The play of the second-last trump gives West more trouble than he can handle. West has to discard a diamond, and the play of the ace and another diamond sets up the twelfth trick.

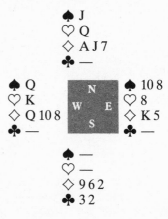

♠ J
♡ Q
♢ A J 7
♣ —

♠ Q
♡ K
♢ Q 10 8
♣ —

♠ 10 8
♡ 8
♢ K 5
♣ —

♠ —
♡ —
♢ 9 6 2
♣ 3 2

It is an example of the three-suit strip-squeeze, unusual in that declarer has a master card in only one of his suits.

9 Profit without Honour

A well-placed trump honour is usually an asset in defence, but bridge is a funny game and there are times when the honour card has to be dropped like a hot potato. If winning a trump trick means conceding two tricks in return, for instance, it is clearly a bad bargain. A defender appreciated this point in the play of the following hand.

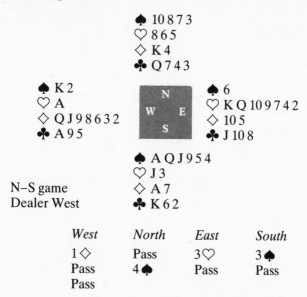

```
              ♠ 10 8 7 3
              ♡ 8 6 5
              ◇ K 4
              ♣ Q 7 4 3

♠ K 2                          ♠ 6
♡ A               N            ♡ K Q 10 9 7 4 2
◇ Q J 9 8 6 3 2  W   E         ◇ 10 5
♣ A 9 5               S        ♣ J 10 8

              ♠ A Q J 9 5 4
              ♡ J 3
N–S game      ◇ A 7
Dealer West   ♣ K 6 2
```

West	North	East	South
1◇	Pass	3♡	3♠
Pass	4♠	Pass	Pass
Pass			

West started with the ace of hearts and switched to the queen of diamonds, which was captured by dummy's king. Since on the bidding the spade finesse could hardly be right, the declarer played the three of spades from dummy and put on his ace. He was pleased when the king of spades dropped on his left, although a little puzzled when West followed with the two of spades on the second round.

Next South turned his attention to the clubs, but he was unable to prevent East from gaining the lead. He thus lost two clubs and two hearts, going one down in his contract.

Do you see what would have happened if West had played the two of spades on the first round? After cashing the ace of diamonds, South would have played a second trump to put West on lead in the position shown in the diagram.

A club return from West permits South to score three club tricks without losing the lead to East. And a diamond return fares no better. South ruffs on the table, discarding a club from hand, and sets up the long club for a discard of his losing heart.

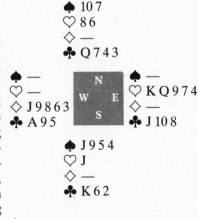

♠ 10 7
♡ 8 6
♢ —
♣ Q 7 4 3

♠ —   ♠ —
♡ —   ♡ K Q 9 7 4
♢ J 9 8 6 3   ♢ —
♣ A 9 5   ♣ J 10 8

♠ J 9 5 4
♡ J
♢ —
♣ K 6 2

In the play of the cards it can sometimes be hard to tell which side should come out on top. Here is a curious hand played in a Hungarian tournament some years ago.

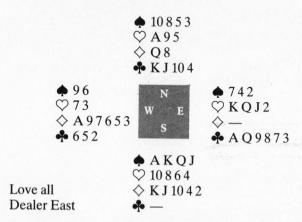

```
                    ♠ 10 8 5 3
                    ♡ A 9 5
                    ◇ Q 8
                    ♣ K J 10 4
    ♠ 9 6                          ♠ 7 4 2
    ♡ 7 3              N           ♡ K Q J 2
    ◇ A 9 7 6 5 3   W   E         ◇ —
    ♣ 6 5 2            S           ♣ A Q 9 8 7 3
                    ♠ A K Q J
                    ♡ 10 8 6 4
Love all            ◇ K J 10 4 2
Dealer East         ♣ —
```

South plays in four spades after East has bid hearts and clubs in canapé fashion. The question is: can South make his contract on best defence?

You could spend a few hours on this since there are many defensive variations, but in fact the declarer has an answer to anything the defenders may try.

A heart lead gives South the hardest task. East is allowed to win the first trick and the heart continuation is won by the ace. Now the declarer must draw trumps since he cannot afford to suffer a diamond ruff, but after three rounds of trumps he has to proceed with care. A diamond lead at this point will not do, for West will go up with the ace and return a club, holding South to nine tricks. Instead, South must concede a second heart to East.

The best East can do at this point is to return the ace of clubs, removing declarer's last trump and leaving the position shown in the diagram.

South counters neatly by leading the jack of diamonds to place West in a dilemma. If West takes his ace of diamonds, dummy's losing clubs are eventually discarded on the ten of diamonds and the established heart.

So West plays low on the jack of diamonds, but this does not help his cause. South's next move is to discard the queen of

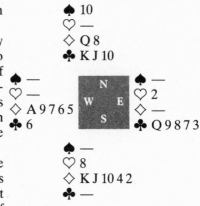

```
              ♠ 10
              ♡ —
              ◇ Q 8
              ♣ K J 10
  ♠ —                    ♠ —
  ♡ —        N           ♡ 2
  ◇ A 9 7 6 5  W   E     ◇ —
  ♣ 6           S        ♣ Q 9 8 7 3
              ♠ —
              ♡ 8
              ◇ K J 10 4 2
              ♣ —
```

diamonds on the winning heart. He then ruffs a diamond in dummy and plays the king of clubs followed by the jack. East wins with the queen but has to concede the last trick to dummy's ten of clubs.

11   The Better Way

There was no swing on this hand from an international match
between Scotland and Wales, but there were some interesting
possibilities in the play.

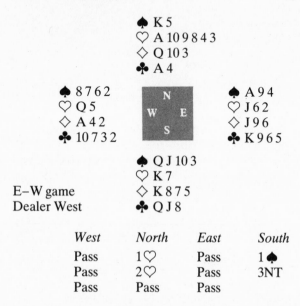

♠ K 5
♡ A 10 9 8 4 3
◇ Q 10 3
♣ A 4

♠ 8 7 6 2
♡ Q 5
◇ A 4 2
♣ 10 7 3 2

♠ A 9 4
♡ J 6 2
◇ J 9 6
♣ K 9 6 5

♠ Q J 10 3
♡ K 7
◇ K 8 7 5
♣ Q J 8

E–W game
Dealer West

West	North	East	South
Pass	1♡	Pass	1♠
Pass	2♡	Pass	3NT
Pass	Pass	Pass	

The bidding was the same in both rooms, as was the opening
lead of a small club. East was allowed to win the first trick with
the king of clubs and his club return went to the ace. The king of
spades knocked out the ace, and a third club was played to
declarer's queen, dummy discarding a heart. On the run of the
spades dummy discarded two more hearts and East his fourth
club, leaving the position shown in the diagram.

Needing two tricks from the diamond suit, the declarers played a low diamond to the ten. East won with the jack, and West eventually scored the diamond ace and the last club to put the contract one down.

The declarers might have done better if they had picked up a small inference from the play. If East had held nothing of value in diamonds he would probably have discarded a diamond rather than a club on

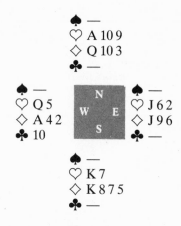

the last spade. The winning play in the diagram position is to lead the king of diamonds from hand. West may take his ace, but if he cashes the winning club he will squeeze his partner in the red suits. It is no better for the defence if West returns a heart or a diamond without cashing the club, for South is then able to set up his ninth trick in diamonds.

One final thought. It was natural for South to bid three no-trumps on the second round and North had no reason to convert to four hearts. But if North *had* played in four hearts he would certainly have made his contract. Although there appears to be a loser in every suit, East cannot profitably attack the clubs and declarer eventually discards his club loser on a long spade or a long diamond.

Conventional methods of showing two-suited hands have a certain merit in competitive auctions but they also have a built-in defect. When the opponents end up playing the hand, the declarer can often make excellent use of information gleaned from the bidding. Here is an example from a pairs tournament.

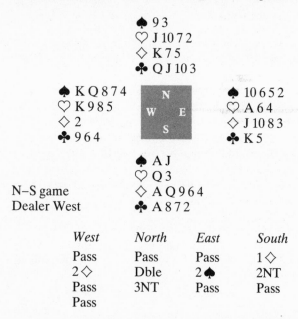

```
                    ♠ 9 3
                    ♡ J 10 7 2
                    ◇ K 7 5
                    ♣ Q J 10 3
    ♠ K Q 8 7 4                      ♠ 10 6 5 2
    ♡ K 9 8 5          N             ♡ A 6 4
    ◇ 2           W         E        ◇ J 10 8 3
    ♣ 9 6 4            S             ♣ K 5
                    ♠ A J
                    ♡ Q 3
N–S game            ◇ A Q 9 6 4
Dealer West         ♣ A 8 7 2
```

West	North	East	South
Pass	Pass	Pass	1◇
2◇	Dble	2♠	2NT
Pass	3NT	Pass	Pass
Pass			

Having kept silent on the first round of bidding, West could not bring himself to pass yet again. His conventional overcall of two diamonds was a Michaels cue bid, showing some values and promising at least nine cards in the major suits. North doubled to indicate that West had stolen his bid, East contested with two spades, and South's rebid of two no-trumps was raised optimistically to game.

West led the king of spades, and when dummy went down South did not think highly of his prospects. To have any chance at all he needed to find the king of clubs with East. Winning the first trick with the ace of spades, he crossed to dummy with the king of diamonds and ran the queen of clubs. East played low and South took the precaution of unblocking the seven from hand. It had occurred to him that it might be useful to have an extra entry in dummy for the later stages.

At trick four the jack of clubs was covered by the king and ace, and the eight of clubs was returned to dummy's ten. Now it was all plain sailing. A diamond came next, and when East played the eight South confidently finessed the nine. West had already contributed four cards in the minor suits and he had promised nine in the majors. It was therefore inconceivable that he had another diamond. When the finesse of the nine of diamonds succeeded, South had five diamonds, four clubs and a spade for a total of ten tricks and a top score.

It would have made no difference if East had inserted the ten or the jack of diamonds on the second round. Thanks to the far-sighted unblocking play in clubs, declarer was in a position to lead the two of clubs to dummy's three and repeat the diamond finesse. But it is most unlikely that this contract would have been made if West had not revealed the secrets of his distribution in the bidding.

13   Uncertain Outcome

On many hands the declarer has to rely on a little help from the defenders. Zoltan Kovacs judged the position correctly on his hand from a Europa Cup match between Hungary and Greece.

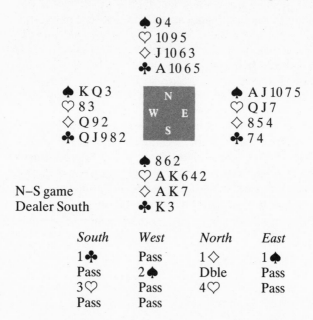

```
                    ♠ 9 4
                    ♡ 10 9 5
                    ◇ J 10 6 3
                    ♣ A 10 6 5
      ♠ K Q 3                       ♠ A J 10 7 5
      ♡ 8 3          N              ♡ Q J 7
      ◇ Q 9 2      W   E            ◇ 8 5 4
      ♣ Q J 9 8 2    S              ♣ 7 4
                    ♠ 8 6 2
                    ♡ A K 6 4 2
N–S game            ◇ A K 7
Dealer South        ♣ K 3
```

South	West	North	East
1♣	Pass	1◇	1♠
Pass	2♠	Dble	Pass
3♡	Pass	4♡	Pass
Pass	Pass		

West led the king of spades and continued with the queen. East overtook with the ace and switched to a diamond. South went up with the ace, cashed the ace of hearts, ruffed his third spade on the table and continued with two more rounds of hearts. In with the queen, East returned a second diamond.

Now declarer faced his moment of truth. The obvious line was to take the finesse, but Kovacs could not believe that East would lead twice away from the queen of diamonds. The only other possibility was a squeeze in the minor suits, so declarer went up with the king of diamonds and cashed another trump to reach the position shown in the diagram.

Sure enough, the play of the last trump caught West in a minor-suit squeeze and the border-line game was made.

Although the declarer made the right decision, he could not have been too certain of the outcome. In these situations much depends on the calibre of the opponents. If East had held the queen of diamonds, it would have been quite a smart move for him to lead the suit twice in an attempt to nudge declarer towards the losing option.

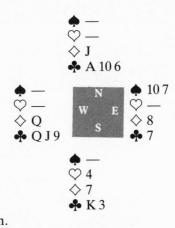

♠ —
♡ —
◇ J
♣ A 10 6

♠ —   ♠ 10 7
♡ —   ♡ —
◇ Q   ◇ 8
♣ Q J 9   ♣ 7

♠ —
♡ 4
◇ 7
♣ K 3

Declarer's line of play presupposed a misdefence on the part of East. This was reasonable enough since few players defend perfectly. East lost his way when in with the ace of spades. He had two spade tricks in the bag and could hope for a further trick in trumps. The setting trick was certainly likely to come from diamonds, but there was no need for an immediate attack on the suit. If East had seen the danger of a minor-suit squeeze against his partner he might have found the right counter. A club switch at trick three and a further club lead at a later stage would have made the declarer's task impossible.

Early unblocking is often the key to success in the play of the cards. Polish star Lesniewski had the chance to show his mettle on this hand from a match between Poland and Bulgaria.

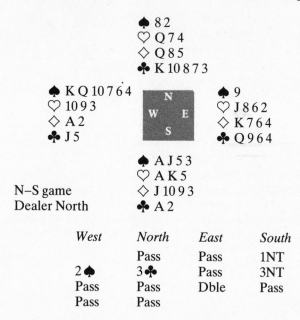

```
              ♠ 8 2
              ♡ Q 7 4
              ◇ Q 8 5
              ♣ K 10 8 7 3

♠ K Q 10 7 6 4              ♠ 9
♡ 10 9 3          N        ♡ J 8 6 2
◇ A 2          W     E     ◇ K 7 6 4
♣ J 5             S        ♣ Q 9 6 4

              ♠ A J 5 3
              ♡ A K 5
N–S game      ◇ J 10 9 3
Dealer North  ♣ A 2
```

West	North	East	South
	Pass	Pass	1NT
2♠	3♣	Pass	3NT
Pass	Pass	Dble	Pass
Pass	Pass		

West led the king of spades and the declarer assessed his chances. It looked as though it would be possible to establish two diamonds, but that added up to only eight tricks. The ninth trick would have to come from one of the black suits, and the prospects in clubs were not very good in view of East's double.

Displaying a high degree of foresight, Lesniewski played the eight of spades from dummy and the three from his own hand. West switched to the ten of hearts and South attacked the diamonds. He regained the lead with the next heart and continued with diamonds to knock out the remaining enemy honour. After winning the third heart, South played off the established diamonds and cashed the top clubs, ending in dummy. This was the position.

The two of spades was played from the table and South covered with the five, forcing West to win and return a spade into the major tenace.

Many players would not have seen the need to unblock the eight of spades at the first trick. If North is left with the eight of spades instead of the two in the diagram position, West can defeat the game by

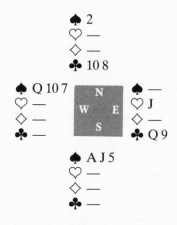

♠ 2
♡ —
♢ —
♣ 10 8

♠ Q 10 7   ♠ —
♡ —   N   ♡ J
♢ —   W   E   ♢ —
♣ —   S   ♣ Q 9

♠ A J 5
♡ —
♢ —
♣ —

underplaying with the spade seven, allowing East to win the last two tricks.

If South *does* fail to play the eight of spades at trick one, he can recover by discarding it on the fourth diamond, winning the second club in hand and exiting with the five of spades. For that matter, South can succeed by winning the first trick with the ace of spades and playing for a similar throw-in ending. But the elegant unblock and Bath coup is somehow more satisfying.

15   Comedy Show

Drop into any bridge club at the end of an individual contest and you are sure to be regaled with hard-luck stories. Most partners, it seems, are uninsurable. The trauma of facing a strange partner (and some of them are very strange) each round is such that many players refuse to enter such events. I think this is carrying matters too far. Individual contests can be great fun as long as they are not taken seriously. Long ago I discovered that the way to handle such events is to treat them as one big joke from start to finish. We are, after all, mere playthings of the Gods.

There must have been laughter on Olympus after the play of the following hand from a masters individual.

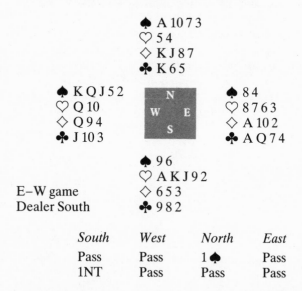

```
                    ♠ A 10 7 3
                    ♡ 5 4
                    ◇ K J 8 7
                    ♣ K 6 5
  ♠ K Q J 5 2          N           ♠ 8 4
  ♡ Q 10          W        E       ♡ 8 7 6 3
  ◇ Q 9 4             S            ◇ A 10 2
  ♣ J 10 3                         ♣ A Q 7 4
                    ♠ 9 6
                    ♡ A K J 9 2
  E–W game          ◇ 6 5 3
  Dealer South      ♣ 9 8 2
```

South	West	North	East
Pass	Pass	1♠	Pass
1NT	Pass	Pass	Pass

The contract was a normal one and I had to find a lead from the West seat. It seems natural to start with the king of spades, or perhaps the jack of clubs, but one of my problems in these situations is that I know too much. Remembering a famous hand where the Australian star, Tim Seres, brought off a coup by underleading the king, queen and jack, I decided to lead the five of spades. It looked quite promising when dummy went down and declarer called for the three. But partner, instead of producing the hoped-for nine, could find nothing better than the eight.

Declarer blinked, as well he might, then won with the nine and played a diamond to the jack and ace. Not taking the opening lead Seresly enough, East returned a low heart to the jack and queen. I continued wryly with the king of spades to dummy's ace, and when the heart ten fell the declarer gratefully took his seven tricks for a top score.

Where the initial lead was the king of spades or the jack of clubs, the contract normally went two down to give East–West a plus score of 100. But note that if East had returned a spade when in with the ace of diamonds, and if declarer had finessed in hearts, as he surely must, the result would have been plus 150 and a top for East and West.

An ambitious slam was reached at both tables on this hand from a team-of-four match.

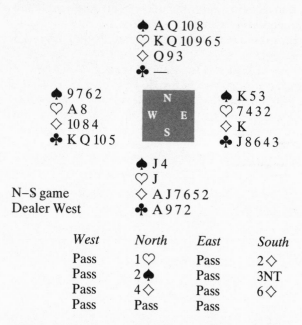

♠ A Q 10 8
♡ K Q 10 9 6 5
◇ Q 9 3
♣ —

♠ 9 7 6 2
♡ A 8
◇ 10 8 4
♣ K Q 10 5

♠ K 5 3
♡ 7 4 3 2
◇ K
♣ J 8 6 4 3

♠ J 4
♡ J
◇ A J 7 6 5 2
♣ A 9 7 2

N–S game
Dealer West

West	North	East	South
Pass	1♡	Pass	2◇
Pass	2♠	Pass	3NT
Pass	4◇	Pass	6◇
Pass	Pass	Pass	

One declarer was given the chance to make his slam when West started with the king of clubs, but he went astray in quite an instructive manner. He ruffed in dummy, played the nine of diamonds to the king and ace, and continued with the jack of hearts. This was not good enough. West took his ace and switched to a spade, ruining declarer's communications. South had no option but to take the spade finesse and the slam went one down.

It seems natural to ruff the first trick in dummy, but the need to preserve control in clubs is an illusion. It is the trump entries in dummy that have to be preserved, and South scuppered his chances when he weakened dummy's trumps at trick one. If he discards a spade from dummy and wins the first trick with the ace of clubs he is much better placed. The jack of hearts comes next, and West is helpless after taking his ace. If he switches to a spade, declarer wins with the ace and plays a low diamond, hoping for a favourable trump position such as actually exists. If instead West continues with a second club, South ruffs in dummy, plays the nine of diamonds to the king and ace, returns to the queen of diamonds, ruffs a heart and draws the last trump. The ace of spades provides access to the winning hearts on the table and the slam is made.

In the other room the declarer had no chance when West found the inspired lead of a spade.

It is worth while taking a quick look at some of the alternative contracts. Game in either red suit is of course a simple proposition, but what about six hearts? This slam will be made unless East finds the double-dummy lead of the king of diamonds.

Three no-trumps should be defeated if the defenders exercise reasonable care. If South holds up the ace of clubs for three rounds, West must switch to a spade and East must switch again to a heart.

The advantages of holding up an ace are fairly well documented and players seldom go wrong at no-trumps. In a suit contract the position is often less clear, but success may still depend on refusing to win at the first opportunity. Here is an example.

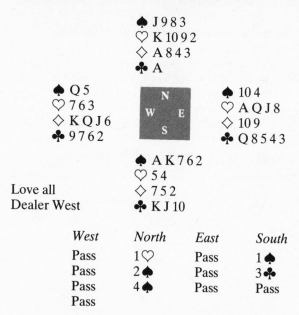

♠ J 9 8 3
♡ K 10 9 2
◇ A 8 4 3
♣ A

♠ Q 5   ♠ 10 4
♡ 7 6 3   ♡ A Q J 8
◇ K Q J 6   ◇ 10 9
♣ 9 7 6 2   ♣ Q 8 5 4 3

♠ A K 7 6 2
♡ 5 4
◇ 7 5 2
♣ K J 10

Love all
Dealer West

West	North	East	South
Pass	1♡	Pass	1♠
Pass	2♠	Pass	3♣
Pass	4♠	Pass	Pass
Pass			

The final contract was reasonable enough, but when West led the king of diamonds and dummy went down the declarer saw that there was a great deal of work to be done. Even if he could manage to avoid the loss of a trump trick, there was an obvious danger of losing two tricks in each of the red suits. After considering the risk of a 5–1 diamond split, South still deemed it wise to hold up the ace on the first round, and from that point onwards the contract was unbeatable.

South won the diamond continuation with the ace, unblocked the ace of clubs, played a spade to the king and ruffed the jack of clubs in dummy. A further spade to the ace took care of the outstanding trumps, and after discarding a diamond on the king of clubs South continued with a heart in the diagram position.

The guess in the heart suit was not too difficult. West was marked with the K-Q-J of diamonds and had produced the spade queen. With the ace of hearts as well he might have opened the bidding, so South put in the nine of hearts from dummy. East won with the jack but was forced to yield a tenth trick to declarer whether he continued with hearts or switched to a club.

On the lie of the cards declarer would have succeeded

```
              ♠ J
              ♡ K 10 9 2
              ◇ 8
              ♣ —
  ♠ —                      ♠ —
  ♡ 7 6 3        N         ♡ A Q J 8
  ◇ J 6      W     E       ◇ —
  ♣ 9            S         ♣ Q 8
              ♠ 7 6 2
              ♡ 5 4
              ◇ 7
              ♣ —
```

even if he had played the king of hearts on the first round, but the play of the nine would have been essential if West had held one of the minor heart honours.

Can four spades be defeated? West may switch to a heart at trick two, but this makes no real difference. Declarer wins the diamond return at trick three, eliminates the black suits, and plays a heart to end-play East as before.

It takes an initial heart lead to defeat the game. After a heart to the nine and jack, a diamond overtaken by West and ducked by declarer, a second heart and a second diamond, the contract has no chance. But who would lead a heart from that West hand?

The late Jean-Michel Boulenger was one of France's most distinguished players. He was a triple European Champion and a member of the fighting French team which lost to the Aces in the final of the 1971 Bermuda Bowl.

Boulenger was a modest and popular champion and, above all, a fine technician. Here is an example of his play.

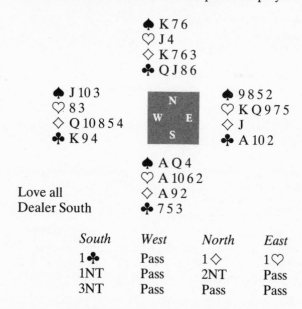

```
                       ♠ K 7 6
                       ♡ J 4
                       ◇ K 7 6 3
                       ♣ Q J 8 6
     ♠ J 10 3                              ♠ 9 8 5 2
     ♡ 8 3               N                 ♡ K Q 9 7 5
     ◇ Q 10 8 5 4    W       E             ◇ J
     ♣ K 9 4              S                ♣ A 10 2
                       ♠ A Q 4
                       ♡ A 10 6 2
Love all               ◇ A 9 2
Dealer South           ♣ 7 5 3
```

South	West	North	East
1♣	Pass	1◇	1♡
1NT	Pass	2NT	Pass
3NT	Pass	Pass	Pass

West led the eight of hearts. How would you plan the play?

It seems natural to play low from dummy in order to make sure of two heart tricks, but look what happens if declarer does this. East puts in the nine of hearts and South has to win with the ten to secure his second heart trick. When declarer plays clubs, as he must, West goes up with the king and continues with hearts, clearing the suit while East still has the ace of clubs as an entry.

Appreciating this danger, Boulenger played the jack of hearts from dummy at trick one and ducked in hand when East covered with the queen. East returned the seven of hearts to declarer's ten. A club was led and West went up with the king, but now he had no heart to return and South was able to develop his ninth trick without difficulty.

The expert declarer constantly aims at making life difficult for the defenders, and Boulenger certainly succeeded on this hand. But astute readers may have noticed that it is really a defensive problem. When a club is led at trick three West should play low, allowing his partner to capture the jack with his ace. On the heart continuation West has the chance to make a name for himself by discarding the king of clubs!

The deadly effect of this discard is seen in the diagram. Declarer needs a second trick from the club suit, but when East comes in with the ten of clubs he is able to cash two further heart winners to put the contract one down.

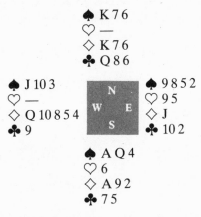

♠ K 7 6
♡ —
♢ K 7 6
♣ Q 8 6

♠ J 10 3
♡ —
♢ Q 10 8 5 4
♣ 9

♠ 9 8 5 2
♡ 9 5
♢ J
♣ 10 2

♠ A Q 4
♡ 6
♢ A 9 2
♣ 7 5

Sensible bidding pays good dividends in the long run, but anyone who expects a fair result on every hand is doomed to disappointment. Justice took a back seat on this hand from an encounter between the two American teams in the 1977 Bermuda Bowl.

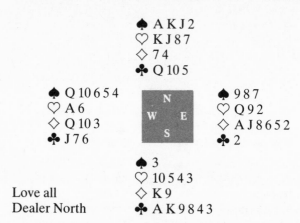

♠ A K J 2
♡ K J 8 7
◇ 7 4
♣ Q 10 5

♠ Q 10 6 5 4
♡ A 6
◇ Q 10 3
♣ J 7 6

♠ 9 8 7
♡ Q 9 2
◇ A J 8 6 5 2
♣ 2

♠ 3
♡ 10 5 4 3
◇ K 9
♣ A K 9 8 4 3

Love all
Dealer North

In one room Bobby Wolff played in the normal contract of four hearts from the North position. East began with the ace and another diamond, and declarer played a heart to the jack and queen. East switched to his singleton club and later obtained a club ruff to put the contract one down.

In the other room Hamilton landed in five no-trumps after a misunderstanding in the bidding.

West	North	East	South
Eisenberg	Passell	Kantar	Hamilton
	1♣	2◇	Dble
4◇	Pass	Pass	4NT
Pass	5◇	Pass	5♡
Pass	5NT	Pass	Pass
Pass			

Four no-trumps was intended as natural but taken as Blackwood, and five hearts was read as a request to bid five no-trumps.

Against this precarious contract West led the three of diamonds (the queen would have been a happier choice). East might have saved the day by allowing declarer to hold the first trick, but he played the ace and another diamond and the last defensive chance had gone. Winning the second diamond, Hamilton ran the clubs to reach the position shown in the diagram.

The play of the last club was agonising for West. What could he discard? The heart ace was out of the question for that would enable declarer to make no fewer than twelve tricks. If the ten of diamonds had been discarded, South would have thrown a spade from dummy

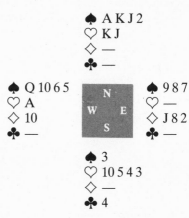

♠ A K J 2
♡ K J
♢ —
♣ —

♠ Q 10 6 5
♡ A
♢ 10
♣ —

♠ 9 8 7
♡ —
♢ J 8 2
♣ —

♠ 3
♡ 10 5 4 3
♢ —
♣ 4

and played either a spade for a finesse or a heart to ensure eleven tricks. In practice West threw a spade, but this was no better. Declarer discarded a heart from dummy and took the spade finesse for eleven tricks anyway.

Try your hand at a defensive problem which came up at a tournament in Greece.

Love all
Dealer South

♠ A 8 5 2
♡ 10 9 7 5
♢ A J
♣ A Q 4

South	West	North	East
1♣	Pass	1♡	Pass
2♡	Pass	2♠	Pass
2NT	Pass	3NT	Pass
Pass	Pass		

♠ Q 10 7
♡ Q 8 3 2
♢ Q 10 3
♣ K J 10

West leads the four of spades, the two is played from dummy and declarer drops the jack under your queen. How do you continue?

Partner appears to have led from a five-card suit headed by the king, which marks declarer with a 1-3-4-5 shape and every missing honour card. Since the picture is clear at trick one we may as well set out the full hand.

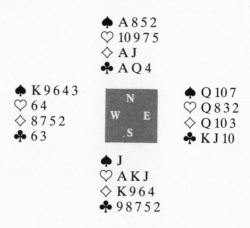

♠ A 8 5 2
♡ 10 9 7 5
♢ A J
♣ A Q 4

♠ K 9 6 4 3
♡ 6 4
♢ 8 7 5 2
♣ 6 3

♠ Q 10 7
♡ Q 8 3 2
♢ Q 10 3
♣ K J 10

♠ J
♡ A K J
♢ K 9 6 4
♣ 9 8 7 5 2

The club finesse is wrong for declarer but the heart finesse is right, and you will not defeat this contract on the normal continuation of the ten of spades. Declarer will hold up until the third round and tackle the clubs, setting up three tricks in that suit to go with his three hearts, two diamonds and one spade.

Is there any hope for the defence? Well, if you reflect that declarer does not know everything, you may decide to try a return of the seven of spades at trick two. This unexpected thrust has a good chance of piercing declarer's defences.

South will discard a diamond, West will put in the nine, and if declarer wins with dummy's ace you will not be able to deny him nine tricks. But, unless you have taken too long to ponder your return, South is unlikely to win the second spade. He will hold up again, and it will be West's turn to think.

West will realise that you must have a powerful motive for blocking the spades, and what can this be but a promotable diamond holding? The diamond switch leaves the defence in control. The jack is covered by the queen and king, and a club finesse loses to the king. Now the play of your low diamond establishes a fifth trick for the defence.

On a double-dummy basis, the only way of defeating the game is for West to start with a diamond and East to switch to the queen of spades when in with the king of clubs. Well, it's not impossible.

Those who consistently reach sensible contracts have a success-ful, if rather a dull, time at the bridge table. It is the play of bad contracts that often generates the most excitement. Here is an example from an international trial.

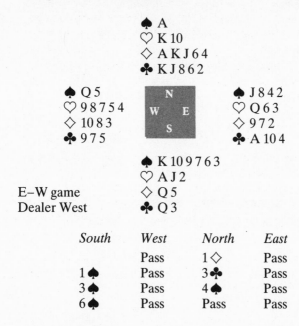

```
                    ♠ A
                    ♡ K 10
                    ◇ A K J 6 4
                    ♣ K J 8 6 2
    ♠ Q 5                          ♠ J 8 4 2
    ♡ 9 8 7 5 4      N             ♡ Q 6 3
    ◇ 10 8 3      W     E          ◇ 9 7 2
    ♣ 9 7 5          S             ♣ A 10 4
                    ♠ K 10 9 7 6 3
                    ♡ A J 2
E–W game            ◇ Q 5
Dealer West         ♣ Q 3
```

South	West	North	East
	Pass	1◇	Pass
1♠	Pass	3♣	Pass
3♠	Pass	4♠	Pass
6♠	Pass	Pass	Pass

North and South were clearly not on the same wave-length. South thought that his partner's force and subsequent raise promised a 3-1-5-4 shape and therefore jumped straight to six spades. If North had rebid three no-trumps or four clubs on the third round, the sound contract of six no-trumps would have been reached.

Against six spades the opening lead was the nine of hearts. Dummy went down and South's eyebrows went up. The ten of hearts was covered by the queen and ace, and a spade to the ace brought small cards from the opponents. Prospects for making the slam looked dismal. The only chance appeared to be to find West with a doubleton spade honour and to run the diamonds through East.

Returning to hand with the queen of diamonds, South cashed the king of spades, dropping the queen from West and discarding a club from the table. A diamond to the jack was followed by the ace of diamonds for a club discard. The king of diamonds was ruffed by East with the eight of spades and over-ruffed by South with the nine. Now a heart to the king put dummy on lead for the play of the last diamond. Whether East ruffed with his master trump or not, the remaining club could be discarded and the slam was made.

The odds against the success of this gruesome slam were pretty high. It required a doubleton trump honour with West, at least three diamonds with East and, for all practical purposes, a heart lead to provide the twelfth trick. Declarer can succeed on a trump lead, it is true, but he is quite likely to go down by attempting the heart finesse the wrong way.

The gambling element in bidding has a great appeal to some players. Look at this hand from a pairs tournament.

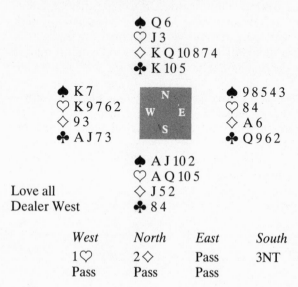

```
                        ♠ Q 6
                        ♡ J 3
                        ◇ K Q 10 8 7 4
                        ♣ K 10 5

        ♠ K 7              N           ♠ 9 8 5 4 3
        ♡ K 9 7 6 2    W       E       ♡ 8 4
        ◇ 9 3              S           ◇ A 6
        ♣ A J 7 3                      ♣ Q 9 6 2

                        ♠ A J 10 2
                        ♡ A Q 10 5
Love all                ◇ J 5 2
Dealer West             ♣ 8 4
```

West	North	East	South
1♡	2◇	Pass	3NT
Pass	Pass	Pass	

In an effort to make up for a previous bad board, South took a flyer at three no-trumps. It's not a bad shot if you have a taste for living dangerously.

West made the happy decision to attack in clubs rather than hearts. On the lead of the three of clubs the five was played from dummy and East won the trick with the nine. At this point the fate of the contract was finely balanced. East decided to return the eight of hearts, which was a perfectly reasonable defence. Declarer clearly could not afford to play low, for on winning the trick West would switch back to clubs, establishing five tricks for the defence.

South therefore rose with the ace of hearts and West followed with the six. When the diamonds were tackled East took his ace on the second round and continued with the four of hearts. South played the five, and West was left with no winning option. If he had played low he would have been ruinously squeezed on the run of the diamonds, so he won with the king and returned the suit. Now declarer had three hearts, five diamonds and the ace of spades for his contract.

It takes a spade switch from East when in with the ace of diamonds to ensure five tricks for the defence. West might have anticipated his partner's problem. If he had played the two of hearts on the first round, East would have had a better chance of finding the killing switch.

The contract can be defeated rather more easily if East continues clubs at trick two instead of switching to a heart. West takes the ace of clubs and clears the suit, and the ace of diamonds is knocked out. East cashes the queen of clubs, and he has to exercise a little care on the next trick. Dummy has had to find a discard on the fourth club and clearly could not spare a diamond. Let's say a spade was discarded from the table. East must follow dummy's discard, switching to a spade, not a heart, after the queen of clubs.

Suppose East returns a heart in the diagram position. This allows declarer to bring off a Vienna Coup. South goes up with the ace of hearts and runs the diamonds to squeeze West

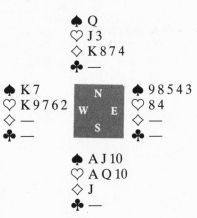

♠ Q
♡ J 3
◇ K 8 7 4
♣ —

♠ K 7　　　　　♠ 9 8 5 4 3
♡ K 9 7 6 2　　♡ 8 4
◇ —　　　　　　◇ —
♣ —　　　　　　♣ —

♠ A J 10
♡ A Q 10
◇ J
♣ —

automatically in the majors. A spade return from East kills all squeeze chances and leaves declarers helpless.

Similarly, if a heart is discarded from dummy on the fourth club, East must switch to a heart, the suit of dummy's singleton.

There is, of course, a more professional way of defending. West can put in the jack of clubs at trick two, allowing dummy's king to win. Now, on gaining the lead with the ace of diamonds, East can switch to either major. On the run of the diamonds West can discard three hearts and the ace of clubs, and no squeeze can operate.

Any writer who records his successes at the bridge table is sure to be accused of blowing his own trumpet. My normal practice is to write up my bad hands and wait for my colleagues to report the good ones. Usually I wait in vain.

Anyway, I have to admit that I could have done better on this interesting three no-trump hand from a match between Scotland and England.

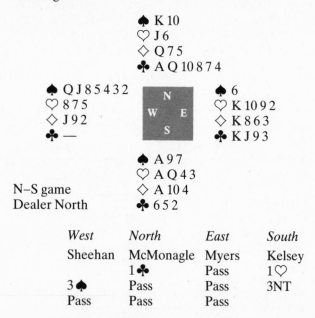

```
                    ♠ K 10
                    ♡ J 6
                    ◇ Q 7 5
                    ♣ A Q 10 8 7 4
 ♠ Q J 8 5 4 3 2          N          ♠ 6
 ♡ 8 7 5             W         E      ♡ K 10 9 2
 ◇ J 9 2                 S            ◇ K 8 6 3
 ♣ —                                 ♣ K J 9 3
                    ♠ A 9 7
                    ♡ A Q 4 3
 N–S game           ◇ A 10 4
 Dealer North       ♣ 6 5 2
```

West	North	East	South
Sheehan	McMonagle	Myers	Kelsey
	1 ♣	Pass	1 ♡
3 ♠	Pass	Pass	3NT
Pass	Pass	Pass	

A double of three spades might have brought in 500 points, but the vulnerable game seemed a reasonable prospect. West led the two of diamonds to the king and ace, and I played a club, ducking in dummy when West discarded a spade. East returned a diamond to his partner's nine, which was allowed to win, and West continued with the jack of diamonds to dummy's queen. Thinking that there was no chance if East held the last diamond, I played another low club from dummy.

East duly produced the thirteenth diamond on which I discarded hearts from both hands. The return of the king of hearts forced out the ace, and I conceded another club to go one down.

It seemed a normal result at the time and indeed it proved to be a flat board. But when a hand is played on Vugraph there is always someone to point out the chances you have missed.

Consider the position at the point where the third round of diamonds is won by dummy's queen.

West is pretty well marked with a 7-3-3-0 shape, and although only seven immediate tricks are available the contract cannot be defeated if East is burdened with the king of hearts.

All I have to do is to remove East's exit card by cashing the king of spades before playing a low club from the table. On the play of the thirteenth diamond I can discard the nine of spades from hand and a club from dummy. Now East is forced to yield an eighth trick by returning a heart. It makes no difference whether he plays the king or a small one. A low heart runs to the jack, the queen is finessed, and the play of the ace of spades squeezes East in hearts and clubs for the ninth trick. That would have been a splendid play to find at the table.

Of course West had been given the chance to break up the position by returning a heart when he was in with the nine of diamonds. To make the hand against any defence after a diamond lead, declarer must allow the king of diamonds to hold the first trick.

In the other room Graham Kirby played three no-trumps from the North hand and received a spade lead to the jack and king. He might have had a chance if he had played a low club from hand, but he led the jack of hearts to the king and ace and the defenders had no difficulty in establishing five tricks.

Lemmings continue to hurl themselves over cliffs into the sea, and a fair number of declarers seem to display the same sort of death-wish. A curious hand was reported from the Minihouse Marathon held in Rotterdam.

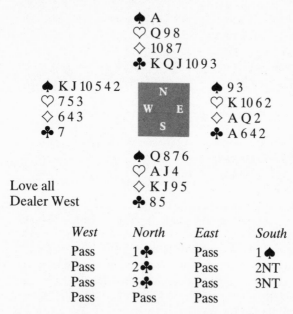

```
                      ♠ A
                      ♡ Q 9 8
                      ◇ 10 8 7
                      ♣ K Q J 10 9 3
   ♠ K J 10 5 4 2          ♠ 9 3
   ♡ 7 5 3                 ♡ K 10 6 2
   ◇ 6 4 3                 ◇ A Q 2
   ♣ 7                     ♣ A 6 4 2
                      ♠ Q 8 7 6
                      ♡ A J 4
   Love all           ◇ K J 9 5
   Dealer West        ♣ 8 5
```

West	North	East	South
Pass	1♣	Pass	1♠
Pass	2♣	Pass	2NT
Pass	3♣	Pass	3NT
Pass	Pass	Pass	

An Indonesian team won the marathon in 1986 and this hand was cited as an example of good Indonesian defence. West led the five of spades, knocking out the only obvious entry for dummy's suit. The declarer played a club to his eight and a club back to the nine and ace. East returned his spade and West overtook to play two more rounds of the suit. South tried a hopeless low heart to the queen and finished three down.

There was nothing wrong with the Indonesian defence, but it seems to me that the nameless declarer might have given the play a better shot. What was he trying to achieve by playing on clubs? The chance of finding a singleton ace was less than 6%, and even then success would not be guaranteed. It must be more sensible to hope for favourable positions in the red suits and try for an end-play against East.

It seems reasonable to play the seven of diamonds from dummy at trick two, running it if East plays low. When the seven wins, declarer continues with the ten of diamonds. East may, of course, take his ace on the first round and return his spade, but this does not present any great problem. Whether West continues spades or switches to something else, South eventually regains the lead and plays a club to dummy. East has to hold up the ace, and declarer finishes the diamonds before playing a second club. This might be the position:

When the second club is played East wins with the ace, but he is forced to yield the rest of the tricks whether he returns a club or a heart. Declarer makes ten tricks in this instance, but he would have been held to nine if West had taken his king of spades before switching to a heart.

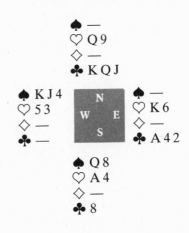

```
              ♠ —
              ♡ Q 9
              ◇ —
              ♣ K Q J
  ♠ K J 4    ┌─────────┐   ♠ —
  ♡ 5 3      │ N       │   ♡ K 6
  ◇ —        │ W     E │   ◇ —
  ♣ —        │    S    │   ♣ A 4 2
             └─────────┘
              ♠ Q 8
              ♡ A 4
              ◇ —
              ♣ 8
```

Ah, you say, but why should East be so helpful as to return his second spade when in with the ace of diamonds? Suppose he returns a diamond, or even a small club to cut the communications with the table.

In both of these cases the answer is the same. After finishing the diamonds, declarer must lead a small spade to break the *defenders'* communications. There is no real risk in this play since South needs to find the spades 6-2 anyway. West will no doubt win the second spade and switch to a heart, which leads to the ending shown in the last diagram.

Now we come to the most interesting variation. Suppose East plays low on the first diamond and inserts the queen on the second round. Declarer continues with a third diamond to knock out the ace, and East takes the chance to make a nuisance of himself by returning a small heart.

This will give declarer an anxious moment or two. After winning in dummy with the eight of hearts, he may play a club to his eight, cash the thirteenth diamond and continue with a spade to cut communications. But on winning with the ten West can play a second heart, destroying the entry potential of dummy's queen. Well, it doesn't much matter for declarer has a simple counter. This is the position:

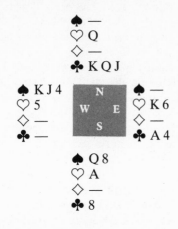

After winning the jack of hearts, South cashes the ace before playing his second club. East scores the ace of clubs and a heart trick, but he has to yield the last trick to one of dummy's clubs. It would have made no significant difference if West had continued with the king and another spade instead of a heart. Now declarer has no need of a second club trick, and East is thrown in to lead away from his king of hearts.

There is another pretty way for declarer to make his contract after a heart return from East at trick five. He can continue hearts for a finesse of the jack and then play the eight of clubs, which East must duck. The position is shown in the new diagram.

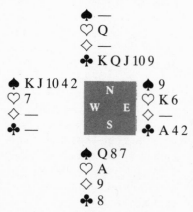

Declarer cashes the heart ace and, if he likes, the remaining diamond. Then he exits with a low spade. If East wins he can cash a heart and the ace of clubs but must then concede the rest to dummy.

If West wins the spade he is forced to yield the ninth trick to declarer in spades.

So the contract was cold all along. Why are we bothering with this hand?

Some problems are best set out under table conditions with only two hands on view. Here is an example from a rubber game where overtricks are supremely unimportant.

♠ A K
♡ A J 5 3
♢ 6 2
♣ Q 7 6 4 2

Game all
Dealer South

	South	West	North	East
	1♡	Pass	2♣	Pass
	2♡	Pass	4♡	Pass
	Pass	Pass		

♠ 9 5
♡ K 10 8 6 4
♢ A Q 7
♣ K 9 3

West leads the four of spades to dummy's ace. How do you plan the play?

It looks like a fairly straightforward exercise in avoidance play. You can afford to lose two clubs as long as you don't lose a trick in each of the red suits. You may be thinking along the lines of drawing a couple of rounds of trumps and then playing a club to your nine in an attempt to keep East off lead.

But the handling of the trumps must be given priority, and if you get the trumps right that play of a club to the nine may not be necessary. You certainly don't want to lose a trump trick to East, so it must be right to cash the ace of hearts at trick two. If both defenders follow with small cards, you should cash the king of spades before continuing with a second heart. If East follows with another low heart, it seems sensible to finesse the heart ten. A winning finesse will solve all your problems, since you will lose no more than two clubs and one diamond.

Suppose the finesse of the ten of hearts loses to the doubleton queen. The lost trick is pretty sure to come back in the wash, for

West will be end-played when in with the queen of hearts. A spade or a diamond return will present you with the game immediately, so West will have to return a club. If he leads a club honour you can play low from both hands to guarantee success.

The full hand could be:

```
              ♠ A K
              ♡ A J 5 3
              ◇ 6 2
              ♣ Q 7 6 4 2

♠ Q 8 7 4 3        N         ♠ J 10 6 2
♡ Q 7          W       E     ♡ 9 2
◇ K 10 8 5 3               ◇ J 9 4
♣ 10               S         ♣ A J 8 5

              ♠ 9 5
              ♡ K 10 8 6 4
              ◇ A Q 7
              ♣ K 9 3
```

To be sure, on this layout you can make the game more easily by following the adage 'eight ever, nine never' and going up with the king of hearts on the second round. But think of all the fun you'd have missed!

When West has a doubleton queen of hearts, your plan can fail only if East has all three club honours and West has the king of diamonds.

On a different lie of the cards things could become tricky. The worst case is where East shows out on the second round of trumps. Now you have to win with the king and play a third trump. If West has nothing in clubs he will no doubt return one, and you will eventually have to bank on the diamond finesse. Holding an honour in clubs, however, West may well return a spade. In that case you must discard a diamond from dummy and ruff in hand. Your main hope now lies in a 3-2 club break, but you can take a small precaution by playing a low club from both hands on the first round, catering for a singleton ace somewhere. If East wins with a low card and returns a diamond, win with the ace and play the king of clubs, banking on the 3-2 division.

For many years the Royal Bols Distillery of Holland awarded a brilliancy prize for the best-played hand of the year. In 1986 the prize went to Ed Manfield of the United States for a hand played in the final of the Rosenblum Cup.

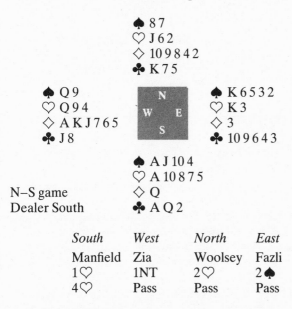

```
                    ♠ 8 7
                    ♡ J 6 2
                    ◇ 10 9 8 4 2
                    ♣ K 7 5
    ♠ Q 9                         ♠ K 6 5 3 2
    ♡ Q 9 4                       ♡ K 3
    ◇ A K J 7 6 5                 ◇ 3
    ♣ J 8                         ♣ 10 9 6 4 3
                    ♠ A J 10 4
                    ♡ A 10 8 7 5
    N–S game        ◇ Q
    Dealer South    ♣ A Q 2
```

South	West	North	East
Manfield	Zia	Woolsey	Fazli
1♡	1NT	2♡	2♠
4♡	Pass	Pass	Pass

Everyone had something to say on this hand. After a normal opening of one heart from South, an unorthodox no-trump overcall from West, a stretched raise from North and a spade bid from East, Manfield launched himself into the precarious heart game.

Zia Mahmoud led the ◇A and continued with the ◇7 (a club or a trump switch is better, as it happens). Fazli ruffed the second diamond with the ♡K, and Manfield had a good idea of the distribution. East seemed likely to have started with K 3 or K 4 in hearts, for with K x x or K 9 he would have ruffed low. And West, marked with six diamonds and three hearts, was likely to have doubletons in both black suits.

Manfield over-ruffed at trick two with the ♡A and found the excellent shot of the ♠J from hand. Zia went in with the ♠Q and continued with the ◇K. Manfield ruffed carefully with the ♡7 and led the ♡5 in the position shown in the diagram.

When Zia played the four of hearts, Manfield backed his reading of the hand by inserting the six from dummy. It all worked out splendidly. Declarer was able to continue with a spade for a finesse of the ten. After cashing the king and ace of clubs he tabled the spade ace, placing West in an impossible position. Whether he ruffed or discarded, Zia could score no more than one trump trick, and Manfield made his ambitious game for a gain of 10 i.m.p.

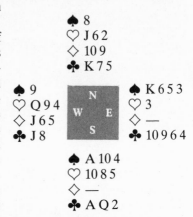

```
            ♠ 8
            ♡ J 6 2
            ◇ 10 9
            ♣ K 7 5
♠ 9                      ♠ K 6 5 3
♡ Q 9 4      N          ♡ 3
◇ J 6 5    W   E        ◇ —
♣ J 8        S          ♣ 10 9 6 4
            ♠ A 10 4
            ♡ 10 8 5
            ◇ —
            ♣ A Q 2
```

Manfield certainly read the position accurately and played the hand with flair, but some judges considered the play to fall just short of brilliance. It was a pity to find that farsighted unblocking play of the ♡7 only to invite defeat by leading the ♡5 at the next trick.

To beat the contract all West had to do was play the queen of hearts and return the four, and I am sure that a less weary Zia would have found this defence. Declarer has to win the heart return in hand, and he has no way of making his remaining trumps separately *and* scoring the five tricks that he needs in the black suits.

What declarer should do, in the diagram position, is continue the good work of unblocking by leading the eight of hearts from hand. Now the contract cannot be defeated. If West plays low the eight of hearts wins, and after a club to the king, a spade for a finesse of the ten, and the ace of clubs, South continues with the ace of spades to trap West's trumps as before.

If West goes up with the queen of hearts and returns the four, declarer is in a position to win in dummy with the six of hearts. The remaining cards are shown in the diagram.

The winning play is now quite straightforward. South ruffs a diamond with the ten of hearts, crosses to dummy with the king of clubs and draws the outstanding trump, discarding the spade four from his hand. A finesse of the ten of spades gives him the rest of the tricks.

```
                ♠ 8
                ♡ J
                ◇ 10 9
                ♣ K 7 5
   ♠ 9                        ♠ K 6 5
   ♡ 9          N             ♡ —
   ◇ J 6 5   W     E          ◇ —
   ♣ J 8        S             ♣ 10 9 6 4
                ♠ A 10 4
                ♡ 10
                ◇ —
                ♣ A Q 2
```

It would have been ideal if Manfield had found this sequence of plays, but most will agree that his actual play was quite brilliant enough to win the prize.

The winkle is a play that sometimes requires a little help from the defenders. Here is an example from a Gold Cup match.

```
              ♠ 9 4 3
              ♡ K J 10 9
              ◇ 9 7 6 3
              ♣ 8 4
♠ K 8 5                        ♠ A Q 7 2
♡ 8 7 6 3         N            ♡ 5 4
◇ K 5         W       E        ◇ 10 8 4 2
♣ 10 7 5 3        S            ♣ K 9 2
              ♠ J 10 6
              ♡ A Q 2
Love all      ◇ A Q J
Dealer South  ♣ A Q J 6
```

	South	West	North	East
	2NT	Pass	3♣	Pass
	3NT	Pass	Pass	Pass

Three clubs was modified Stayman and the rebid showed a hand that was 3-3 in the majors.

West led a heart and the trick was won by dummy's nine. A diamond was played for a losing finesse, and West had his last chance. A spade switch would have netted four more tricks for the defenders, but this was far from obvious at the table. In practice West adopted the passive course of continuing with a second heart.

That was all the help declarer needed. He won with the ace, played off the top diamonds and continued with two more rounds of hearts. East was forced to part with two spades and South also discarded a spade. After a successful finesse of the queen of clubs the position was as shown in the diagram.

Reading the lie of the cards accurately, declarer exited with a spade. West played low and East did his best by winning with the ace. When the ten of diamonds was cashed South discarded his low club, and East had little option but to continue with the queen of spades.

```
            ♠ 9 4 3
            ♡ —
            ♢ 9
            ♣ 8
♠ K 8 5                    ♠ A Q
♡ —         N              ♡ —
♢ —       W   E            ♢ 10
♣ 10 7        S            ♣ K 9
            ♠ J 10
            ♡ —
            ♢ —
            ♣ A J 6
```

The defenders had come to the end of the road. West could permit his partner's queen of spades to hold, in which case South would make the last two tricks in clubs, or he could overtake with the spade king and concede the game-going trick to the nine of spades.

It's quite an amusing ending—from declarer's point of view at any rate.

Television is not a medium that lends itself easily to the presentation of bridge. The action is too slow for all but the committed and there is no prospect of reaching mass audiences as do the ball games. Nevertheless, televised bridge contests do provide compulsive viewing for keen players.

Here is an interesting deal from one of these shows.

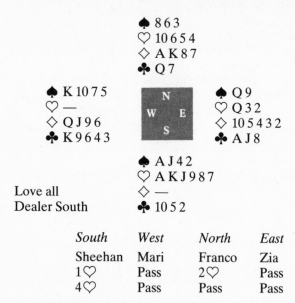

```
                    ♠ 8 6 3
                    ♡ 10 6 5 4
                    ♢ A K 8 7
                    ♣ Q 7
      ♠ K 10 7 5                      ♠ Q 9
      ♡ —            N                ♡ Q 3 2
      ♢ Q J 9 6    W   E              ♢ 10 5 4 3 2
      ♣ K 9 6 4 3    S               ♣ A J 8
                    ♠ A J 4 2
                    ♡ A K J 9 8 7
Love all            ♢ —
Dealer South        ♣ 10 5 2
```

South	West	North	East
Sheehan	Mari	Franco	Zia
1♡	Pass	2♡	Pass
4♡	Pass	Pass	Pass

An initial spade lead, or a club lead and a spade switch, would have given the declarer no chance, but Mari chose the natural lead of the queen of diamonds. Sheehan cashed the top diamonds, discarding spades from his hand. Then, not being gifted with second sight, he played a heart to his ace. On discovering the bad break he continued with a club. West went up with the king and played a second club to his partner's ace. A diamond came back, but the hand was over. Declarer ruffed the diamond, ruffed his third club in dummy and took the marked trump finesse to bring home the game.

The commentator applauded Sheehan's decision to discard spades rather than clubs on the diamonds, but he failed to point out that the contract could have been defeated in spite of this.

It looks normal for West to rise with the king of clubs in case declarer is trying to steal a trick with the queen, but it was not the right move on this occasion. If Mari had played low, Zia would have won and switched to the queen of spades. Declarer does best to hold up, but he has to take his ace on the next round. When a second club is played, West can win with the king to leave the position shown in the diagram.

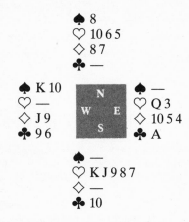

Now a third round of spades is played. Declarer has to ruff in hand, while East has the chance to discard the ace of clubs! The fact that South's ten of clubs is established is supremely unimportant. With no way of reaching dummy, declarer has to concede a trick to the queen of hearts.

Climbing to three no-trumps with a combined count of 22 points is not to be recommended. Here is an amusing hand from an international match between Scotland and Wales.

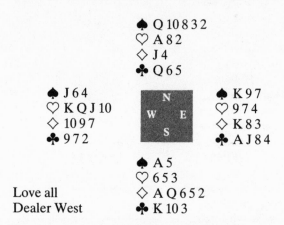

♠ Q 10 8 3 2
♡ A 8 2
◇ J 4
♣ Q 6 5

♠ J 6 4
♡ K Q J 10
◇ 10 9 7
♣ 9 7 2

♠ K 9 7
♡ 9 7 4
◇ K 8 3
♣ A J 8 4

♠ A 5
♡ 6 5 3
◇ A Q 6 5 2
♣ K 10 3

Love all
Dealer West

In one room, after three passes and a weak no-trump from South, North transferred to spades and the Welsh were happy to score 110. There was more excitement in the other room.

West	North	East	South
Hamilton	Silverstone	Stephens	Shenkin
Pass	Pass	1◇	Pass
1♡	Pass	Pass	Dble
Pass	1♠	Pass	1NT
Pass	3NT	Pass	Pass
Pass			

East opened in third position with one diamond, and a bidding misunderstanding propelled the Scots into a hazardous no-trump game. But the play's the thing.

Hamilton attacked in hearts and Shenkin held up the ace until the third round. He then played a spade to his ace and continued with a spade to the ten and king. No return looked attractive to Stephens, who eventually tried a low diamond. This ran to dummy's jack and the winning spades were cashed, South discarding two diamonds and a club. A finesse of the diamond queen was followed by the ace of diamonds, after which a club was established as declarer's ninth trick.

A passive spade return would have served East no better. The run of the spades would then have reduced everyone to the position shown in the diagram.

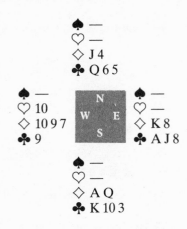

After finessing the queen of diamonds and cashing the ace, South can play a club to the queen and score two club tricks on the return.

It is not too easy to see that the winning defence for East is to return a low club when he is in with the king of spades. If declarer wins with the ten, he cannot reach dummy to cash the spades. If he wins on the table with the queen of clubs and runs the spades, he cannot finesse in diamonds *and* make sure of a second club trick.

Mind you, declarer need not have given East this chance to shine. He might have played a club to his ten before tackling the spades. The contract would then have been unbeatable.

And West had his chance at trick three. If he switches to the ten of diamonds, his partner is off the hook.

When the opponents bid high on distributional values it is usually right for the defenders to attack in trumps. This hand from Dr George Rosenkranz's excellent book on trump leads contains a lesson that was not fully explained by the author.

```
                    ♠ J 6 4
                    ♡ Q 10 8 4 3
                    ◇ A 8 4 2
                    ♣ 6
    ♠ 9 8 3            N            ♠ 5
    ♡ A 9 5        W       E        ♡ K J 7 2
    ◇ J 6 3            S            ◇ K Q 7 5
    ♣ K 8 4 3                       ♣ Q J 9 2
                    ♠ A K Q 10 7 2
                    ♡ 6
Love all            ◇ 10 9
Dealer South        ♣ A 10 7 5
```

South	West	North	East
1♠	Pass	2♠	Dble
4♠	Dble	Pass	Pass
Pass			

West reasoned that this was a good occasion for a trump lead since his partner was marked with strength in the other three suits. Declarer won the lead of the nine of spades in hand and ran the nine of diamonds to East's queen. Seeking to put his partner in for another trump lead, East tried the return of a club. South won with the ace and had an easy cross-ruff for ten tricks.

Should East have returned a heart instead of a club? West certainly thought so, explaining that his double of four spades must surely indicate two key cards, either the ace-king of clubs or the ace of hearts and one club honour. And with the former holding West would probably have led a top club rather than a trump.

This argument is not entirely convincing, and East might have replied that it did not really matter what he returned since West had already scuppered the defence with his opening lead. Suppose East returns a heart to the ace at trick three and West continues with a second trump. Declarer can win as cheaply as possible on the table and play the queen of hearts, discarding a club when East covers with the king. When dummy regains the lead with either the ace of diamonds or the third trump, the ten of hearts is played and East's jack is ruffed out. Declarer thus scores two heart tricks and does not need a club ruff to make his contract.

To give the defence the best chance of defeating the game, West should lead the *three* of spades initially. When leading from three small trumps the lowest card is almost invariably the right choice.

Even with all four hands exposed it can sometimes be hard to see where the game-going trick can come from. On this deal from a rubber bridge game in Italy, however, the declarer solved his problem neatly at the table.

```
                    ♠ K 6
                    ♡ 10 8 6
                    ◇ 9 6 5 2
                    ♣ A Q J 7
  ♠ Q 10 3 2                        ♠ A J 8 4
  ♡ 4              N                ♡ Q J 9
  ◇ K 10 7 3    W     E             ◇ A Q J 8 4
  ♣ 10 8 4 3        S               ♣ 9
                    ♠ 9 7 5
                    ♡ A K 7 5 3 2
Game all            ◇ —
Dealer West         ♣ K 6 5 2
```

West	North	East	South
Pass	Pass	1◇	1♡
Dble	Pass	1♠	2♡
3◇	3♡	Pass	4♡
Pass	Pass	Pass	

The bidding seems more than a little strange. Having made a light-weight negative double and persuaded his partner to bid spades, West supported the wrong suit on the next round. It takes an immediate attack in clubs to defeat a contract of four spades. In practice South would be likely to start with a top heart, after which declarer has an easy time. Five diamonds can also be made on a heart lead.

At any rate, West found the only way to give declarer a problem in four hearts. He led his singleton trump and the nine forced out the king. This seemed to put paid to any idea of ruffing a spade in dummy, for East was likely to have the ace of spades and he would return a trump each time he gained the lead. It looked as though South would have to lose three spades and a heart.

But the declarer, Italian champion Norberto Bocchi, had other ideas. East was marked with a 4-3-5-1 shape, and South saw that he would have a chance if the singleton club was the eight, nine or ten. After cashing the ace of hearts to check the trump position, he played the king of clubs and overtook with dummy's ace. The fall of the nine from East was encouraging. South ruffed a diamond and played a second club, finessing the seven when West played low. East could not afford to ruff with his master trump, for that would enable South to ruff a spade in dummy after all. So East discarded, and South continued with a diamond ruff, a club, another diamond ruff and a fourth club to reach the diagram position.

The last diamond was played from the table and South scored his tenth trick with a ruff.

What happened, in effect, was that declarer created an extra entry to dummy which enabled him to bring off a complete dummy reversal. He took his six trump tricks and his four clubs and left the defenders to fight over the rest of the tricks. It's an easy game, isn't it?

```
              ♠ K 6
              ♡ 10
              ♢ 9
              ♣ —
♠ Q 10 3    N       ♠ A J
♡ —       W   E     ♡ Q
♢ K         S       ♢ Q
♣ —                 ♣ —
              ♠ 9 7 5
              ♡ 7
              ♢ —
              ♣ —
```

Declarer's play cannot be faulted, but such hands hold forth the promise of gold for the keen analyst who never takes anything for granted. I was soon at work with my pencil, sifting and panning, looking for pay-dirt in the form of an alternative line of play. Was it really necessary, I wondered, to overtake the king of clubs with the ace on the first round? Would not a partial dummy reversal followed by a throw-in achieve the same result? A quick check showed that the throw-in does not work since West controls the fourth round of diamonds. However, it takes only a few minor changes in the hand to produce the interesting situation I was thinking about.

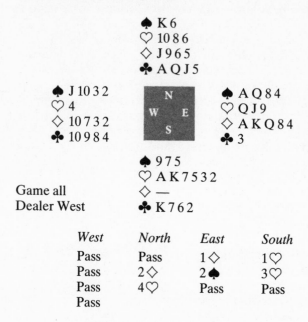

♠ K 6
♡ 10 8 6
◇ J 9 6 5
♣ A Q J 5

♠ J 10 3 2
♡ 4
◇ 10 7 3 2
♣ 10 9 8 4

♠ A Q 8 4
♡ Q J 9
◇ A K Q 8 4
♣ 3

♠ 9 7 5
♡ A K 7 5 3 2
◇ —
♣ K 7 6 2

Game all
Dealer West

West	North	East	South
Pass	Pass	1◇	1♡
Pass	2◇	2♠	3♡
Pass	4♡	Pass	Pass
Pass			

Now four spades has little chance, while four hearts is still in jeopardy on a trump lead. South wins with the king, cashes the ace to confirm the trump position, and faces the same problem of avoiding the loss of four tricks in the majors. Overtaking the club king with the ace doesn't work this time, and in any case there is no need for such pyrotechnics. The contract is cold on the reasonable assumption that East has the top diamonds along with the ace of spades.

South cashes the king of clubs and continues with a club to the jack. As before, East cannot ruff without permitting a spade ruff in dummy. South ruffs a diamond, plays a club to the queen, ruffs another diamond and plays his last club to the ace in the diagram position.

East has already thrown two spades, and if he parts with another one declarer can simply exit with the low spade, setting up a trick for dummy's king.

So East elects to discard a diamond on the last club, but it doesn't help him. South ruffs a diamond and exits with his last trump to enforce the throw-in. After cashing his remaining diamond and the ace of spades, East has to yield the last trick to the spade king.

```
              ♠ K 6
              ♡ 10
              ◇ J 9
              ♣ A
  ♠ J 10 3    ┌─────┐    ♠ A Q
  ♡ —         │  N  │    ♡ Q
  ◇ 10 7      │W   E│    ◇ A K 8
  ♣ 10        │  S  │    ♣ —
              └─────┘
              ♠ 9 7 5
              ♡ 7 5
              ◇ —
              ♣ 6
```

Do you see what happened? The play of the last club squeezed East in three suits, one of which was trumps. It's a variation of the Knockout Strip-Squeeze.

32　Too Strong

Burdened with an over-active imagination, I sometimes dwell on what might have happened rather than what actually happened at the bridge table. I was intrigued by a report about this hand from the Lederer Memorial Trophy some years ago.

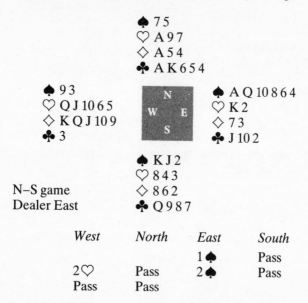

♠ 7 5
♡ A 9 7
◇ A 5 4
♣ A K 6 5 4

♠ 9 3
♡ Q J 10 6 5
◇ K Q J 10 9
♣ 3

♠ A Q 10 8 6 4
♡ K 2
◇ 7 3
♣ J 10 2

♠ K J 2
♡ 8 4 3
◇ 8 6 2
♣ Q 9 8 7

N–S game
Dealer East

West	North	East	South
		1♠	Pass
2♡	Pass	2♠	Pass
Pass	Pass		

The hand was presented as a defensive problem. After a club to the king and a spade back to the queen and king, the defenders lost their way and allowed the contract to be made. North has to keep both his red aces for the second round to make sure of six tricks for the defence.

No mention was made of the contracts reached at the other tables, and I wondered if some intrepid pair might have produced this auction.

West	North	East	South
		1♠	Pass
2♡	Pass	2♠	Pass
Pass	Dble	Pass	3NT
Dble	Pass	Pass	Pass

Liking the look of his spade honours, South takes a flyer at three no-trumps. West doubles and leads the king of diamonds. Declarer allows this to win, takes the ace of diamonds on the second round, plays a spade to his jack, crosses to the king of clubs and plays another spade. This time East takes his ace and counter-attacks with the king of hearts. Declarer wins with the ace, plays a club to his queen and cashes the spade king. Alas, the blockage in clubs prevents him from scoring the five club tricks that he needs and the contract goes one down.

One can imagine the recriminations as North examines his partner's cards. 'Where did you find that three no-trump bid? You're not nearly strong enough.'

'Too strong, you mean,' growls South. 'With the two of clubs instead of the seven I'd have made it.'

33   Cut and Run

In the pairs game a defender often has to take a hard decision about his trick target. Should he try for the maximum or take what he can and run? Experience has taught me that it usually pays to run, but sometimes it is possible to hedge one's bet. On this hand a defender took a far-out position and, as usual, was rewarded with a bottom score.

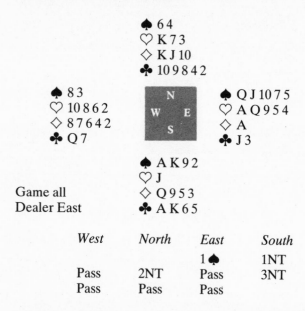

```
                     ♠ 6 4
                     ♡ K 7 3
                     ◇ K J 10
                     ♣ 10 9 8 4 2
      ♠ 8 3                        ♠ Q J 10 7 5
      ♡ 10 8 6 2      N            ♡ A Q 9 5 4
      ◇ 8 7 6 4 2   W   E          ◇ A
      ♣ Q 7           S            ♣ J 3
                     ♠ A K 9 2
                     ♡ J
Game all            ◇ Q 9 5 3
Dealer East          ♣ A K 6 5
```

West	North	East	South
		1♠	1NT
Pass	2NT	Pass	3NT
Pass	Pass	Pass	

South had a difficult bid over one spade and few will quarrel with his overcall of one no-trump. East could not quite find the courage to mention his hearts at the three-level, and West naturally led a spade against three no-trumps.

South captured the ten with his king and played on diamonds. In with the ace, East had to decide whether to continue the spade attack or switch to hearts. Eventually he opted for a low heart, reasoning that this would put the contract two down if his partner had a club stopper.

The heart switch was not a success. After winning a surprise trick with the heart jack, South cashed three diamonds, discarding the small heart from dummy, and then ran the clubs. East was caught in a major-suit squeeze and the declarer made twelve tricks for a top score.

It is the self-inflicted wounds that are the hardest to bear. East was betting on a rank outsider when he switched to a heart at trick three. It was unrealistic to try for a two-trick defeat. In the unlikely event of partner having a club trick, the contract would still be defeated on the prosaic continuation of the queen of spades. On gaining the lead in clubs West would have little choice but to switch to hearts, and the defenders would score two hearts plus a trick in each of the other suits.

As the cards lie there is no chance of defeating the contract, but the spade continuation would have ensured three tricks for the defence and a reasonable score for East and West.

Note that even an initial heart lead is not enough to defeat three no-trumps. East may play three rounds of hearts, but declarer can counter with five rounds of clubs, catching East in a three-suit strip-squeeze. In order to keep guards in spades and diamonds East has to part with a winning heart, after which it is safe for South to knock out the ace of diamonds.

Three no-trumps is by far the most popular contract on border-line game hands, and it is easy to understand why. The path of the defenders is full of pitfalls, and even when an effective defence is present there is a good chance that it will not be found. Here is an example of the sort of thing that happens all the time.

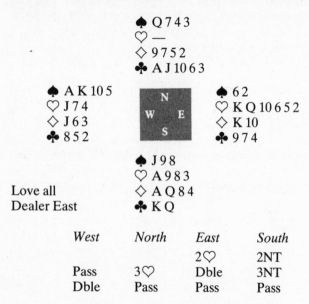

```
                        ♠ Q 7 4 3
                        ♡ —
                        ◇ 9 7 5 2
                        ♣ A J 10 6 3
        ♠ A K 10 5                      ♠ 6 2
        ♡ J 7 4         N              ♡ K Q 10 6 5 2
        ◇ J 6 3       W   E            ◇ K 10
        ♣ 8 5 2         S              ♣ 9 7 4
                        ♠ J 9 8
                        ♡ A 9 8 3
Love all                ◇ A Q 8 4
Dealer East             ♣ K Q
```

West	North	East	South
		2♡	2NT
Pass	3♡	Dble	3NT
Dble	Pass	Pass	Pass

After a weak two hearts from East, three no-trumps was reached at a number of tables in a pairs contest. The contract was not always doubled but it was invariably made on the nose.

West led the four of hearts to his partner's queen, and East returned a low heart to the jack, two diamonds being discarded from the table. Declarer won the third heart, throwing a spade from dummy this time, and played five rounds of clubs, discarding two diamonds and the heart from his hand. The tempo was in declarer's favour, and after setting up a spade winner he was able to take nine tricks with the help of the diamond finesse.

Do you see how the defenders could have done better? That third round of hearts was a mistake. If East switches to a low diamond at trick three the tempo swings the other way. Now the defenders can establish a diamond trick before the declarer can set up his spade.

That's all very well in theory, but at the table it is another matter. One of the West players *did* switch to a diamond at trick three, and the declarer took his only remaining chance by calmly playing the four under East's king. Time stood still while East pondered his return. Eventually he continued with his second diamond and the declarer had his nine tricks.

A simple finesse is a straight fifty-fifty chance, and in theory all such finesses are equal. In practice some are more equal than others, as the declarer discovered on this hand from a pairs event.

♠ 8 7 4 3
♡ 7 4
♢ K Q 8 3
♣ A Q 3

♠ Q 9 5   ♠ J 10 6
♡ A 8 2   ♡ Q J 10 9 5 3
♢ 4   ♢ 7
♣ K 10 8 6 5 2   ♣ J 9 4

♠ A K 2
♡ K 6
Game all   ♢ A J 10 9 6 5 2
Dealer South   ♣ 7

South	West	North	East
1♢	Pass	3♢	Pass
4NT	Pass	5♢	Pass
6♢	Pass	Pass	Pass

South took an optimistic view in the bidding, blasting into a poor slam. West led the five of spades to the ten and king, and South calculated that he needed to find both the ace of hearts and the king of clubs well placed—roughly a 25% chance. After drawing trumps with a diamond to the king, he shrugged his shoulders and played a heart from dummy. His fate quickly became apparent when the defenders took their two heart tricks.

South thought he was unlucky, but on opening the score-slip he discovered that most declarers had made twelve tricks in diamonds, including a couple of others who had bid the slam. Had they received the favourable lead of the ace of hearts? No, they had simply assessed the situation more accurately and had taken the right finesse.

The trouble with playing on hearts is that, even when the ace is with East, declarer needs the club finesse as well if he is to make the slam. The club finesse is no more likely to succeed than the heart finesse, but it carries the bonus of an extra chance when it does succeed. There is now the possibility of doing something with the spades, in which case a heart trick may not be needed. After a winning club finesse, declarer throws his losing spade on the ace of clubs, plays a spade to his ace and returns to dummy with a trump. A spade ruff reveals the happy 3-3 split, and a losing heart is eventually discarded on the thirteenth spade.

Playing on clubs rather than hearts increases the chance of success from 25% to 34%. It's still better not to bid such slams.

Card play is largely a matter of routine, and I am always grateful to a declarer who finds an original way of making his contract. Here is an example from a contest between the Nordic nations.

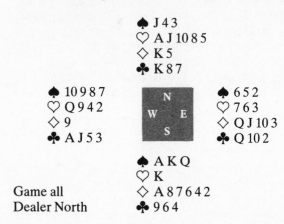

♠ J 4 3
♡ A J 10 8 5
◇ K 5
♣ K 8 7

♠ 10 9 8 7
♡ Q 9 4 2
◇ 9
♣ A J 5 3

♠ 6 5 2
♡ 7 6 3
◇ Q J 10 3
♣ Q 10 2

♠ A K Q
♡ K
◇ A 8 7 6 4 2
♣ 9 6 4

Game all
Dealer North

Everyone played in three no-trumps from one side or the other and the normal lead was a spade. Clearly the game can be made by setting up the hearts, relying on the king of clubs as a late entry to dummy. A number of players adopted this prosaic approach and duly emerged with nine tricks. In the match between Iceland and the Faroes, however, Sigurdur Sverrisson found a more interesting line of play.

Winning the spade lead with the queen, Sverrisson played a low diamond from hand and played low from dummy when West produced the nine. Perhaps he was hoping that East would have to win, in which case the contract would be cold on a normal 3-2 diamond break. West's nine held the trick, however. The low club switch went to the queen, and East continued with the ten of clubs to dummy's king. Three more kings were cashed in quick succession—the king of diamonds, the king of hearts and the

king of spades—to leave the
position shown in the diagram.

West has already thrown a
heart on the second diamond,
and he can find no suitable discard when the ace of diamonds
is played. He is caught, in fact,
in a most unusual type of strip-
squeeze. If West parts with a
spade or a club, South cashes
the ace of spades and then exits
with his club. After taking his
two tricks in the black suits
West has to yield two hearts to
dummy at the end.

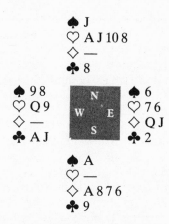

♠ J
♡ A J 10 8
◇ —
♣ 8

♠ 9 8
♡ Q 9
◇ —
♣ A J

♠ 6
♡ 7 6
◇ Q J
♣ 2

♠ A
♡ —
◇ A 8 7 6
♣ 9

It might seem as though West can escape his fate by discarding
a heart on the ace of diamonds, but this is an illusion. After a
heart discard declarer exits immediately with his club, presenting
West with a new losing option. If he cashes his second club trick,
South unblocks the ace of spades and the spade jack becomes an
entry for the good hearts on the table. If West refuses to cash the
thirteenth club, returning a spade instead, South wins and exits in
diamonds to enforce a heart return from East.

It's quite a spectacular ending, but East could have given
declarer a harder time by switching back to spades after winning
the queen of clubs. The position is shown in the new diagram.

It looks natural to test the diamonds now, but if declarer does this he will be defeated, losing two diamonds, two clubs and a spade. And it is too late to try to set up the hearts, for this will also lead to the loss of five tricks.

The only way for declarer to succeed in the diagram position is to lead a club immediately. If West plays the three or the jack, the same ending as before will be developed. If West plays the ace

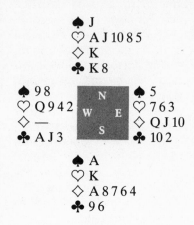

of clubs and returns, say, a spade, South cashes the kings of diamonds, clubs and hearts, and then plays the ace and another diamond to end-play East.

The Caransa tournament in Amsterdam has always been a fruitful source of good material. Here is an interesting hand from the 1987 event.

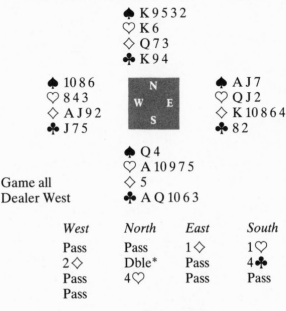

```
                    ♠ K 9 5 3 2
                    ♡ K 6
                    ◇ Q 7 3
                    ♣ K 9 4
    ♠ 10 8 6           N          ♠ A J 7
    ♡ 8 4 3        W       E      ♡ Q J 2
    ◇ A J 9 2          S          ◇ K 10 8 6 4
    ♣ J 7 5                        ♣ 8 2
                    ♠ Q 4
                    ♡ A 10 9 7 5
Game all            ◇ 5
Dealer West         ♣ A Q 10 6 3
```

West	North	East	South
Pass	Pass	1◇	1♡
2◇	Dble*	Pass	4♣
Pass	4♡	Pass	Pass
Pass			

* competitive

Five clubs would have been an easier contract, but the declarer had to struggle in four hearts when his partner gave false preference. West led the ace of diamonds and continued with the jack, which was covered by the queen and king and ruffed by South. The declarer saw that he would be a trick short if he played three rounds of trumps and suffered a further force in diamonds. So he tried to steal a spade trick first by playing a club to the king and returning a low spade from dummy. But East was having none of that. He rose with the ace of spades and played another diamond, reducing declarer to three trumps.

The outlook was not too hopeful, but South cashed the queen of spades and continued with the ace and queen of clubs. East could not afford to ruff the third club at the cost of his natural trump trick, so he discarded his remaining spade to leave the position shown in the diagram.

A fourth club was led and West was put to the test. If he discards his spade, declarer can discard from dummy to make sure of four of the remaining five tricks.

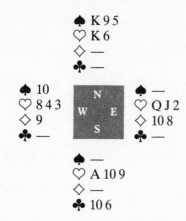

If West discards his diamond, however, the defenders can make two tricks whether South ruffs or discards in dummy. Suppose South discards. East ruffs and returns a diamond, and West's uppercut with the eight of hearts promotes a second trump trick for the defence.

In practice West decided that it would be a good idea to ruff the fourth club with the eight of hearts. This defence was not good enough. Declarer over-ruffed with the king and played a spade, ruffed high by East and over-ruffed by South. Now the fifth club could be ruffed with dummy's six of hearts to make sure of a tenth trick.

Declarer played well up to a point, but the contract could have been made without relying on misdefence by West. South does better to cash the ace and queen of clubs without first releasing the queen of spades. When East refuses to ruff the third club the position is as shown in the new diagram.

It is clear that East must have both of the missing trump honours, and South can make sure of his contract by overtaking the queen of spades with the king and continuing with another spade.

If East ruffs low, South over-ruffs, ruffs a club with the king of hearts and plays another spade to score his ten of hearts

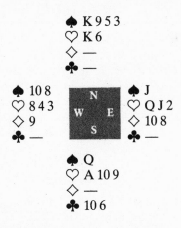

en passant. If East ruffs the third spade high, South discards a club and cannot be prevented from making the rest of the tricks.

On some hands it can be hard to decide whether the declarer or the defenders should come out on top. Would you choose to play this four-spade contract or defend against it?

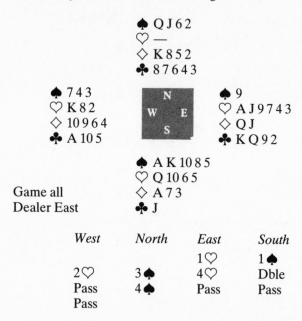

♠ Q J 6 2
♡ —
♢ K 8 5 2
♣ 8 7 6 4 3

♠ 7 4 3
♡ K 8 2
♢ 10 9 6 4
♣ A 10 5

♠ 9
♡ A J 9 7 4 3
♢ Q J
♣ K Q 9 2

♠ A K 10 8 5
♡ Q 10 6 5
♢ A 7 3
♣ J

Game all
Dealer East

West	North	East	South
		1♡	1♠
2♡	3♠	4♡	Dble
Pass	4♠	Pass	Pass
Pass			

Naturally West does best to start with a trump. This prevents declarer from ruffing three hearts in dummy and he has to try to establish his tenth trick in clubs. Winning the first trick in hand, South plays the jack of clubs. West takes his ace and continues with a second trump which is won in dummy. South may now ruff a club, ruff a heart, ruff a club and ruff another heart. Having only one trump left, South cannot afford to ruff the fourth club. Instead he discards a heart or a diamond on the fourth club, but East plays the ace and another heart, establishing the setting trick for his partner's seven of spades.

Can declarer do better? Perhaps. The timing is more favourable if he concedes a club to East at an earlier stage. After winning the second trump and playing a club from the table, South should view East's card with special interest. If East plays the nine South has to ruff, for he cannot afford to lose the trick to West and have a trump come back. South continues with a heart ruff and another club. This time East has to play the king or the queen, and South discards a diamond to leave this position:

South wins the diamond return with the ace, ruffs another heart and ruffs another club. After drawing the last trump, he is able to cross to dummy with the king of diamonds and cash the established club as his tenth trick.

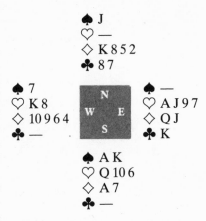

Does this mean that the declarer should always prevail? Not so. The defenders can have the last word if East is smart enough to play the king or the queen of clubs under West's ace. East cannot then be forced to win any round of clubs except the fourth one, and the game must be defeated.

To have a little fun give your partner the East hand. At the end of the play you can ask innocently why he or she did not drop a high club under your ace at trick two.

A curious position arose in the play of the following hand from an international match between Scotland and England some years ago.

♠ Q 10 7 6
♡ K 9 5 4 3
◇ 9 4 3
♣ 7

♠ 9 2
♡ 8 2
◇ K Q 8 7 6
♣ 9 8 6 4

♠ K 8 5 3
♡ A 10 6
◇ 10 5 2
♣ K J 5

♠ A J 4
♡ Q J 7
◇ A J
♣ A Q 10 3 2

E–W game
Dealer North

West	North	East	South
	Pass	Pass	1♣
Pass	1♡	Pass	3NT
Pass	Pass	Pass	

Four hearts is clearly a better contract, but the Scots played in three no-trumps and the declarer was off to a good start when West led the six of diamonds to the ten and jack. The next two tricks were won by the queen and jack of hearts, East sensibly refusing to part with his ace. The jack of spades was also allowed to win, and South then got off lead with his third heart. The writing was on the wall, however. When back in with the ace of diamonds the declarer had nowhere to go. All he could do was to play the ace and another spade, and the defenders took their five tricks to put the contract one down.

There is a line of play to make the game, however, and I leave it to the reader to decide whether it smacks too much of the midnight oil. The key move is to overtake the jack of spades with dummy's queen at trick four. Now East cannot afford to hold up his king of spades. If he does, South can switch to clubs and make ten tricks with the aid of the finesse.

So East takes his king of spades immediately and returns a diamond to knock out the ace. Now it is natural for South to test the spades, cashing the ace and continuing with a spade to the ten. When the suit fails to break, he throws West in by leading the nine of diamonds in the diagram position.

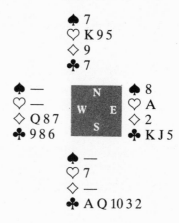

What can West do? He cannot refuse to win the diamond trick or South will finesse in clubs for the two tricks he needs. If West finishes the diamonds, he inflicts a fratricidal squeeze on his partner. Finally, if West switches to a club before running the diamonds, South wins economically and exits with his heart, making sure of two further tricks on the enforced club return.

40   *Exit Card*

It is not often that a defender has to make a critical discard at trick one, but it happened on this hand from rubber bridge.

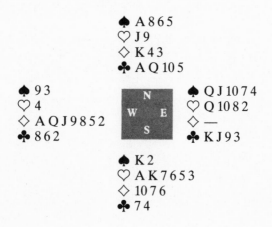

Love all
Dealer West

♠ A 8 6 5
♡ J 9
♢ K 4 3
♣ A Q 10 5

West	North	East	South
3◇	Pass	Pass	3♡
Pass	Pass	Pass	

♠ Q J 10 7 4
♡ Q 10 8 2
♢ —
♣ K J 9 3

West leads the ace of diamonds against South's contract of three hearts. Choose a discard from the East hand.

Does this strike you as a trivial problem? It is usually right to keep length with dummy in such situations, and it looks automatic to discard a spade on the ace of diamonds. That is what East did in practice, but the story did not have a happy ending for him. Here is the full hand.

♠ A 8 6 5
♡ J 9
♢ K 4 3
♣ A Q 10 5

♠ 9 3
♡ 4
♢ A Q J 9 8 5 2
♣ 8 6 2

♠ Q J 10 7 4
♡ Q 10 8 2
♢ —
♣ K J 9 3

♠ K 2
♡ A K 7 6 5 3
♢ 10 7 6
♣ 7 4

West continued with the queen of diamonds at trick two and dummy's king was ruffed away. Declarer won the spade return with the king, cashed the top trumps, then played a spade to the ace and ruffed a spade before exiting with a trump. East cashed the jack of spades but declarer simply discarded his losing diamond, leaving East to concede the ninth trick by leading into the club tenace.

Was this ending foreseeable? I believe it was, and if East had peered into the future he might have found the right discard at trick one. East can count on one diamond and two trumps for the defence, and he knows that the contract will be defeated if he can score two tricks in the black suits. He expects to be on lead twice, which means that he will be able to knock out the spade entry in dummy to remove any chance of declarer setting up a second club trick by ruffing. He should therefore throw a club on the ace of diamonds, retaining his fifth spade as an exit card.

You see the difference this makes? Declarer may still discard his losing diamond on the fourth spade, but the fifth spade forces him to ruff and try the losing club finesse.

In 1987 the Lederer Memorial Trophy was won by the Swedish international team. In the match between Sweden and a team representing London, an interesting position developed on this hand when Roman Smolski found himself playing in an unlikely contract.

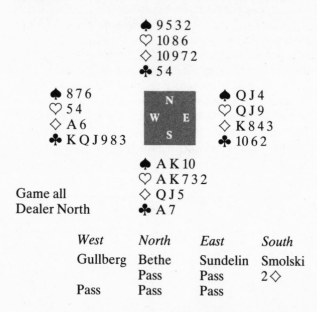

♠ 9 5 3 2
♡ 10 8 6
♢ 10 9 7 2
♣ 5 4

♠ 8 7 6
♡ 5 4
♢ A 6
♣ K Q J 9 8 3

♠ Q J 4
♡ Q J 9
♢ K 8 4 3
♣ 10 6 2

♠ A K 10
♡ A K 7 3 2
♢ Q J 5
♣ A 7

Game all
Dealer North

West	North	East	South
Gullberg	Bethe	Sundelin	Smolski
	Pass	Pass	2♢
Pass	Pass	Pass	

Smolski opened a 'multi' two diamonds, showing either a weak two in hearts or a balanced 21-22. He really didn't expect to play there, but Henry Bethe sensibly judged that two diamonds was likely to be as good a spot as any for his side.

Gullberg led the king of clubs, which was allowed to hold the first trick. Smolski won the second club, cashed the top cards in both major suits and then exited with a spade to East. Sundelin cashed the queen of hearts and switched to the three of diamonds in the position shown in the diagram.

At this point Smolski found the key play of inserting the jack of diamonds. West won and returned the six of diamonds which was covered by dummy's seven.

East had three options, none of which was any good. If he played the king of diamonds and continued with a small one, South would unblock the queen and win the last three tricks on the table. If East played the four of diamonds on the second round, declarer would

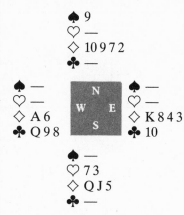

```
            ♠ 9
            ♡ —
            ◇ 10 9 7 2
            ♣ —
♠ —                      ♠ —
♡ —      N               ♡ —
◇ A 6  W     E           ◇ K 8 4 3
♣ Q 9 8      S           ♣ 10
            ♠ —
            ♡ 7 3
            ◇ Q J 5
            ♣ —
```

ruff the thirteenth spade and score a further trump trick in dummy. And finally, if East chose to cover the seven of diamonds with the eight, South would win with the queen and ruff a heart on the table. East cannot gain by discarding, and if he over-ruffs he is bound to concede the last two tricks whether he returns his club or a trump.

Note that it was essential for South to insert a high diamond on the first round. If he plays low, the defenders play three rounds of the suit and East eventually scores the setting trick with the diamond eight.

That was highly competent play by the declarer, but East missed a difficult chance to defeat the contract. If he switches to a trump before cashing the queen of hearts, he can hold declarer to seven tricks by covering dummy's seven of diamonds with his eight on the second round.

It helps to have a plentiful supply of entries when you are playing the cards. When there is difficulty in crossing from one hand to the other, the simplest of contracts can become a bit of a nightmare. In this contract of three no-trumps the declarer had to make an unusual play to bring in nine tricks.

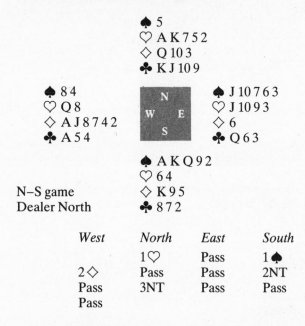

♠ 5
♡ A K 7 5 2
◇ Q 10 3
♣ K J 10 9

♠ 8 4
♡ Q 8
◇ A J 8 7 4 2
♣ A 5 4

♠ J 10 7 6 3
♡ J 10 9 3
◇ 6
♣ Q 6 3

♠ A K Q 9 2
♡ 6 4
◇ K 9 5
♣ 8 7 2

N–S game
Dealer North

West	North	East	South
	1♡	Pass	1♠
2◇	Pass	Pass	2NT
Pass	3NT	Pass	Pass
Pass			

South might have taken the money by doubling two diamonds. Best defence against this contract will net 500, but the lure of the vulnerable game proved too strong. Against three no-trumps West found that awkward lead of the queen of hearts.

South could hope to win three spades and two tricks in each of the other suits, although the shortage of entries in his own hand was likely to prove a handicap. He ducked the opening lead, won the heart continuation with the ace and tackled the clubs by leading the king from dummy. West took his ace and switched to the eight of spades, East's ten drawing the queen. A second club went to the nine and queen, and East returned the jack of hearts. South discarded a spade and West a diamond as dummy won with the king. The jack of clubs drew the remaining cards in the suit, and this was the position with the lead in dummy:

South could afford to lose only one more trick, and he was faced with the difficult problem of how to return to hand to cash his winning spades. He realised that it would be a mistake to cash the last club at this point, since there was no discard he could spare from his hand. Instead, he played the ten of diamonds from dummy and covered it with his king.

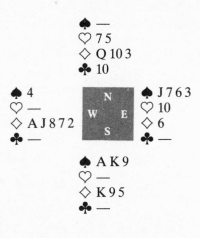

♠ —
♡ 7 5
♢ Q 10 3
♣ 10

♠ 4
♡ —
♢ A J 8 7 2
♣ —

♠ J 7 6 3
♡ 10
♢ 6
♣ —

♠ A K 9
♡ —
♢ K 9 5
♣ —

Now West was helpless. If he ducked, South would cash the top spades, discarding hearts from the table, and continue with a diamond towards the queen. And if West took the ace of diamonds he would have to provide South with a ninth trick whether he returned a diamond or a spade.

Unblocking is often the key to success in the play of the cards.
Look at this hand from a six-table pairs contest.

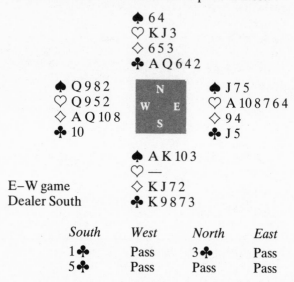

```
                    ♠ 6 4
                    ♡ K J 3
                    ◇ 6 5 3
                    ♣ A Q 6 4 2
   ♠ Q 9 8 2                       ♠ J 7 5
   ♡ Q 9 5 2          N            ♡ A 10 8 7 6 4
   ◇ A Q 10 8      W     E         ◇ 9 4
   ♣ 10                S           ♣ J 5
                    ♠ A K 10 3
                    ♡ —
E–W game            ◇ K J 7 2
Dealer South        ♣ K 9 8 7 3
```

South	West	North	East
1♣	Pass	3♣	Pass
5♣	Pass	Pass	Pass

Five clubs by South was the standard contract and the normal
lead was the two of spades to the jack and king. Most of the
declarers relied entirely on finding one of the diamond honours
favourably placed. After drawing trumps they played a diamond
from dummy and put in the jack. West won with the queen and
switched to a low heart, and eventually the declarers had to lose
two further diamond tricks for one down.

At one table the declarer found a subtle way of giving himself
an extra chance. Winning the first trick with the king of spades,
he played the seven of clubs to the queen in dummy and returned
the three of hearts. East did the right thing by playing low, but he
was unable to avoid the small hesitation that gave away the
position of the ace. South ruffed with the club eight and played
the nine of clubs to dummy's ace, West discarding a heart. Next
came a small diamond to the jack and queen.

Unable to return a diamond or a spade without loss, West had to play the nine of hearts. The jack was played from dummy and East's ace was ruffed with the king of clubs. South continued with the precious three of clubs to dummy's six, West discarding a spade and East a heart. On the next two trumps East discarded a spade and a heart, South a spade and a diamond, and West the queen of hearts and the eight of diamonds, leaving the position shown in the diagram.

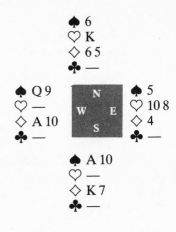

♠ 6
♡ K
♢ 6 5
♣ —

♠ Q 9   ♠ 5
♡ —   ♡ 10 8
♢ A 10   ♢ 4
♣ —   ♣ —

♠ A 10
♡ —
♢ K 7
♣ —

The inference that West was guarding tenaces in both spades and diamonds was overwhelming, so declarer cashed the king of hearts and threw his small diamond. West had to bare the diamond ace and was subsequently thrown in to concede the last two tricks in spades.

If East had gone up with the ace of hearts at trick three, the play would naturally have been a great deal easier.

One of the most interesting hands of the 1987 European Championships at Brighton came from the match between Denmark and Iceland.

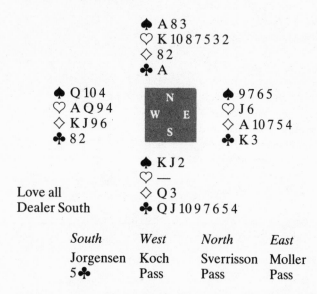

♠ A 8 3
♡ K 10 8 7 5 3 2
♢ 8 2
♣ A

♠ Q 10 4
♡ A Q 9 4
♢ K J 9 6
♣ 8 2

♠ 9 7 6 5
♡ J 6
♢ A 10 7 5 4
♣ K 3

♠ K J 2
♡ —
♢ Q 3
♣ Q J 10 9 7 6 5 4

Love all
Dealer South

South	West	North	East
Jorgensen	*Koch*	*Sverrisson*	*Moller*
5♣	Pass	Pass	Pass

In the other room the Danes had played in three clubs, making an overtrick for a score of 130, but in this room Jorgensen was more ambitious. Was it going to be 5 i.m.p. to Denmark or 7 to Iceland?

Faced with a difficult choice of lead, Dennis Koch settled for the ace of hearts, regretting it as soon as he saw dummy. Declarer ruffed the ace of hearts, crossed to the table with the ace of clubs, discarded a diamond on the king of hearts and ruffed a third heart in hand. Then he exited with the queen of clubs to East's king.

It looks natural for East to cash the ace of diamonds at this point, but Steen Moller looked deeply into the position and saw that this might expose his partner to a major-suit squeeze. After winning with the king of clubs, therefore, he switched at once to a spade. This proved to be the killing defence. South might have won with the king and attempted to rectify the count by conceding a diamond, but East would have won and sent back another spade to snuff out the squeeze. In practice South decided to rely on the spade finesse and the contract went quietly one down.

That was an excellent and far-sighted defence by East, but the declarer had missed a small opportunity at trick four. Instead of ruffing the third heart he might have discarded the queen of diamonds. West cannot attack the spades from his side of the table, and the option of the squeeze instead of the finesse remains intact.

Given the choice, would you prefer a fair 6-1 trump fit or a weakish 4-3? Most players would settle for the 6-1, I imagine, but it was the 4-3 that came out ahead on this hand from a Gold Cup match.

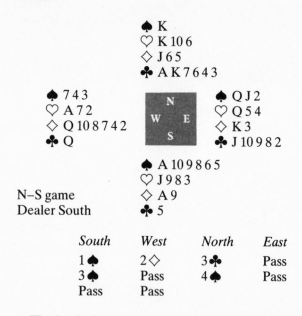

♠ K
♡ K 10 6
◇ J 6 5
♣ A K 7 6 4 3

♠ 7 4 3
♡ A 7 2
◇ Q 10 8 7 4 2
♣ Q

♠ Q J 2
♡ Q 5 4
◇ K 3
♣ J 10 9 8 2

♠ A 10 9 8 6 5
♡ J 9 8 3
◇ A 9
♣ 5

N–S game
Dealer South

South	West	North	East
1♠	2◇	3♣	Pass
3♠	Pass	4♠	Pass
Pass	Pass		

The lead of the queen of clubs went to dummy's ace. South unblocked the king of spades, then continued with the king of clubs for a diamond discard. West ruffed, and the declarer had to lose a further trump and two hearts for one down.

Even at double-dummy there is no way for South to make ten tricks in spades. He may, after unblocking the spade king, ruff a club with the eight of spades and continue with the ace and another spade, but the defence prevails when East returns his low diamond. West wins with the queen, and his heart switch establishes two more tricks for the defence before the diamonds can be unblocked.

In the other room South saw no reason to suppress his second suit.

South	West	North	East
1♠	2♢	3♣	Pass
3♡	Pass	4♡	Pass
Pass	Pass		

The lead was again the queen of clubs, and declarer did not think much of his prospects. Winning with the ace, he unblocked the spade king and continued with the ten of hearts from the table. It did not occur to East to play the queen, and West refused to part with his ace. Suddenly things looked a lot brighter. Next came the king of clubs for a diamond discard. West ruffed, cashed the ace of hearts and switched to a diamond, but declarer was in control. He won with the diamond ace, cashed the ace of spades, ruffed a spade with the king of hearts, ruffed a club back to hand and played winning spades, allowing East to score the queen of hearts when he chose. South lost three trumps but nothing more.

An initial diamond lead—or the ace of hearts and a diamond switch—defeats four hearts by taking out South's outside entry before the king of spades has been unblocked. After the lead of the queen of clubs, however, there is no defence.

Suppose East goes in with the queen of hearts on the first round and continues trumps. That's no good. South wins the third trump in dummy, takes a diamond discard on the king of clubs, plays a diamond to his ace and concedes a spade, losing just one spade and two trumps.

What if West switches to diamonds after two rounds of trumps? South ruffs a spade with the king of hearts and plays the king of clubs for a diamond discard. West may ruff (South makes an overtrick if he doesn't), but there is nothing more for the defence. If East switches to diamonds after taking the queen of hearts, South wins with the ace, ruffs a spade with the king of hearts and continues trumps. In this variation the defenders make two trumps and a diamond.

Finally, if both defenders duck on the first round of hearts,

West may refuse to ruff the king of clubs, discarding a spade instead to leave the position shown in the diagram.

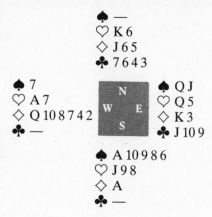

♠ —
♡ K 6
◇ J 6 5
♣ 7 6 4 3

♠ 7
♡ A 7
◇ Q 10 8 7 4 2
♣ —

♠ Q J
♡ Q 5
◇ K 3
♣ J 10 9

♠ A 10 9 8 6
♡ J 9 8
◇ A
♣ —

Now South cannot expect to establish the spades, but he can hope to succeed on cross-ruff lines. After a diamond to the ace and the ace of spades, he plays another spade. If West ruffs with the heart seven, South over-ruffs and plays a trump, establishing the spades after all. If West discards, South ruffs low in dummy, ruffs a diamond in hand, ruffs a further spade with the king of hearts and plays the jack of diamonds. West cannot gain by ruffing a spade with the ace of hearts, nor can East gain by ruffing the third diamond with the queen of hearts, so ten tricks roll in.

When faced with a seemingly impossible task, too many declarers abandon hope and cut their losses. Faith is at a discount in our society and few players believe in miracles. Yet the pack of cards is steeped in magic, and the most ordinary hand can be influenced by powerful unseen forces. Miracles are all around for those who have the eyes to see them. As Francis Thompson put it:

> The angels keep their ancient places;
> Turn but a stone, and start a wing!
> 'Tis ye, 'tis your estranged faces,
> That miss the many-splendoured thing.

The flutter of wings in the background went unnoticed by the declarer on this hand from a Gold Cup match.

```
               ♠ A K 5 2
               ♡ A 5
               ◇ A 8 7 6 3
               ♣ 6 4
♠ 10 9 8 6 3                    ♠ J
♡ Q 4 2          N             ♡ J 9 8 6
◇ Q J 10 5    W     E          ◇ K 2
♣ A              S             ♣ J 9 8 7 5 3
               ♠ Q 7 4
               ♡ K 10 7 3
               ◇ 9 4
               ♣ K Q 10 2
```

Game all
Dealer North

West	North	East	South
	1◇	Pass	1♡
Pass	1♠	Pass	2NT
Pass	3NT	Pass	Pass
Pass			

West led the ten of spades to dummy's ace, and at trick two a low diamond was played from the table. East went in with the king and returned a club to the king and ace. West switched back to spades, South winning with the queen as East discarded a club. A diamond was ducked to West and a third spade knocked out the king, East throwing another club. The diamond ace was then cashed, both East and South discarding hearts.

When the diamonds failed to break the declarer threw in the towel. He might have tried for an eighth trick by taking the club finesse, but this entailed some risk of going three down and South had no wish to enter minus 300 on his score-card. He settled for minus 200 by cashing the top hearts and the queen of clubs. This translated to a loss of 9 i.m.p., for in the other room South had played quietly in one no-trump and had been allowed to make three overtricks.

But consider what might have happened in three no-trumps if a more determined declarer had been at the wheel. This was the position when the diamond ace had been cashed:

South finesses the ten of clubs and West can safely discard the three of spades. The next play of the queen of clubs forces West to part with a heart. A diamond is thrown from dummy, and when South continues with the two of clubs the pressure on West becomes unbearable. No matter whether he discards his master

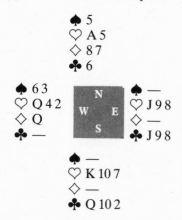

spade, his master diamond or a heart, declarer can make the rest of the tricks on the forced heart return.

What sort of an ending was that? Technically it can be described as a compound guard squeeze incorporating a losing squeeze card. East is subjected to a strip-squeeze in clubs and hearts, and the moment of the throw-in operates the guard squeeze against West.

It is not necessary to have a full understanding of such endings in order to produce them at the table. All that is needed is a stout heart and the determination to succeed. The cards will always forgive a lack of comprehension more readily than a failure of courage.

There is no effective defence against the no-trump game on the lie of the cards. West cannot afford to switch to hearts when in with the second diamond; he has to continue spades in order to prevent the establishment of a long diamond. East might switch to hearts at trick three, but this is no better. If he plays the six of hearts, South's seven forces out the queen. If East plays the nine of hearts to the ten, queen and ace, declarer can play on clubs himself and East is eventually end-played to yield an extra trick in hearts.

47   Trial and Error

From a bridge writer's point of view the best hands are those that develop into a battle of wits between the declarer and the defenders. When there are many variations to take into account it can be hard to determine which side should come out on top. The most complex examples can be regarded as 52-card double-dummy problems.

Consider this hand from a league match.

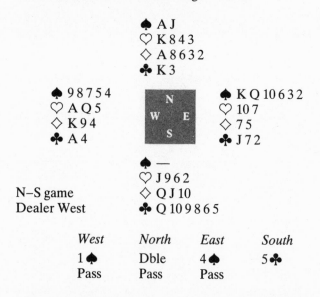

```
                    ♠ A J
                    ♡ K 8 4 3
                    ♢ A 8 6 3 2
                    ♣ K 3
     ♠ 9 8 7 5 4              ♠ K Q 10 6 3 2
     ♡ A Q 5         N        ♡ 10 7
     ♢ K 9 4      W     E     ♢ 7 5
     ♣ A 4          S         ♣ J 7 2
                    ♠ —
                    ♡ J 9 6 2
  N–S game          ♢ Q J 10
  Dealer West       ♣ Q 10 9 8 6 5
```

West	North	East	South
1♠	Dble	4♠	5♣
Pass	Pass	Pass	

Four spades was going down, of course, but this was not obvious at the time and it seemed reasonable for you to bid.

West led a spade against five clubs and you saw that there were likely to be communication problems. You would have liked to take some time for analysis, but in a league match you can't sit for ever without playing a card. So you played the ace of spades on which East flamboyantly dropped the king. This told you where the rest of the high cards were likely to be, but it didn't seem to help very much. You discarded a heart from hand and played the

112

king of clubs from the table. West won with the ace and returned a second spade for you to ruff.

You continued with the queen of diamonds followed by the jack. If West had covered on the first or second rounds, you would have been able to draw trumps with the help of a finesse, clear the diamonds, and use the king of hearts as an entry to the long diamonds. But West did the right thing by playing low on the first two rounds of diamonds. There was then no winning path for you. The play of a third diamond or a heart would inevitably allow the defenders to score a diamond ruff, so you simply cashed the queen of clubs in the hope that the jack would drop. No luck: one down.

Thinking about the result later that evening you are not altogether happy with your line of play. It looks as though there should be some way of making five clubs, and you subject the hand to some heavy analysis.

Instead of playing the king of clubs from dummy at trick two you might try the low club for an immediate finesse of the ten. No, that doesn't work. West wins and plays another spade, and after unblocking the club king you have no way back to hand to draw the last trump.

Well, what about playing the jack of spades from the table at trick one, ruffing in hand and playing a club. West has to go up with the ace, and if he returns a club to dummy's king you are home. You can ruff the ace of spades, draw the remaining trump and play on diamonds. But, of course, West will continue with a spade after taking the ace of clubs. This ruins the timing and leaves you in the same losing position as before.

Ah, but suppose you unblock the king of clubs under the ace. Now West can't afford to return a spade, for this would enable you to finesse in trumps and achieve a winning position. The best West can do is return a low diamond which runs to your ten. Is there a counter to that?

At this point the jack of hearts from your hand is an interesting shot. If West plays low your troubles are over. You simply play a diamond to the ace, discard your third diamond on the spade ace, draw trumps with the aid of a finesse and play on hearts. Suppose West covers your jack of hearts with the queen. This takes out the entry for the long diamonds but it does not destroy your chances. After winning with the king of hearts you draw trumps with a finesse, clear the diamonds and exit with a heart in the diagram position.

If East wins the heart he has to put you back in dummy to enjoy the diamonds, while if West wins he sets up the hearts for you.

So it seems that West must play the ace when you lead the

```
              ♠ A
              ♡ 8 4
              ◇ 8 6
              ♣ —
♠ 8 7 5    N        ♠ K 10 6 3
♡ A 5   W     E     ♡ 10
◇ —                 ◇ —
♣ —        S        ♣ —
              ♠ —
              ♡ 9 6 2
              ◇ —
              ♣ 9 8
```

jack of hearts from hand. If he returns a spade you can throw a diamond from hand, draw trumps with a finesse and ruff out the diamonds to establish eleven tricks. But West will not be so kind as to return a spade after taking his ace of hearts. He will continue with his low heart to dummy's king. Now you can finesse in trumps or set up the diamonds, but you can't do both.

This is frustrating, for you are convinced that there must be a way of making five clubs. Suppose you throw a diamond on the ace of spades and then play the low club for a finesse of the ten. West is likely to return a club to the king. Now you can ruff the jack of spades, draw the last trump and lead the queen of diamonds, but West will defeat you by covering with the king to block the suit.

All right, let's try discarding a diamond on the ace of spades, ruffing the jack of spades in hand and playing the queen of diamonds. West does best to cover, and after winning with the ace you can return to the jack of diamonds and play a club to West's ace. A club, heart or spade return at this point lets you home, but again West has a way of frustrating you. He returns the nine of diamonds. After ruffing this and playing a club to the king, you can return to hand only by destroying one of your diamond winners which leaves you a trick short.

Still, we seem to be drawing ever closer to a solution. For a final attempt let's try ruffing the first spade in hand and leading the queen of diamonds. If West plays low, you continue with a trump to his ace. On a spade return you discard a diamond, unblock the king of clubs and play the ace and another diamond, ruffing in hand. Now it is just a matter of drawing the last trump and playing a heart towards the king.

West may cover the queen of diamonds with his king at trick two, but this time you have an answer. After winning with the ace you return the low club for a finesse of the ten. Now it doesn't matter what West tries. If he plays another diamond to your ten, you cross to the king of clubs, ruff the ace of spades, draw the outstanding trump, unblock the diamonds and play a heart.

That's it! You knew all along that there was a way of making five clubs. Why didn't you find it at the table?

On this hand from an individual contest a dubious slam was reached at a couple of tables.

```
              ♠ K 4
              ♡ A 3
              ◇ A J 10 8
              ♣ A K 10 8 3
♠ Q 6 3                        ♠ A 9 8 2
♡ Q 7          N               ♡ J 4
◇ Q 9 4     W     E            ◇ K 7 6 5 3
♣ Q 9 7 6 2    S               ♣ J 5
              ♠ J 10 7 5
              ♡ K 10 9 8 6 5 2
Love all      ◇ 2
Dealer North  ♣ 4
```

West	North	East	South
	2NT	Pass	6♡
Pass	Pass	Pass	

A slightly stretched two no-trumps was the popular opening on the North hand. Most of the South players were content to bid four hearts, but two were in a gambling mood and took a flyer at six. It is a ridiculous slam, of course, but one declarer scrambled home when a spade was led. The other was defeated after a club lead.

The double-dummy analysis is complicated and I am not going to bore you with the full details. You can either explore the variations for yourself, or take my word for it that six hearts can be made on any lead except a club.

After a club lead the play takes an interesting turn if declarer wins with the ace, ruffs a low club at trick two and advances the jack of spades. West has to cover with the queen to give the defence a chance, and East must capture the king with his ace. If

East returns a stolid spade at this point, declarer can win with the ten, draw trumps ending in dummy, cash the king of clubs for a spade discard, ruff a club in hand and run the trumps to produce the ending shown in the diagram.

When the eight of hearts is played neither defender is able to keep two diamonds and the slam is made.

After winning with the ace of spades at trick three, East has only one good card to re-

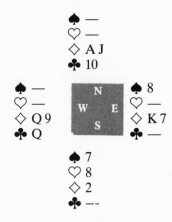

♠ —
♡ —
◇ A J
♣ 10

♠ —   ♠ 8
♡ —   ♡ —
◇ Q 9   ◇ K 7
♣ Q   ♣ —

♠ 7
♡ 8
◇ 2
♣ —

turn—the king of diamonds. This removes dummy's outside entry, breaking up the double squeeze position and ensuring the defeat of the slam.

An intriguing hand made an appearance at the 1988 North American Spring Nationals. In the Men's Pairs Bob Hamman had to defend against an optimistic contract of four spades.

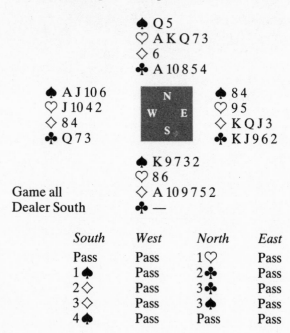

♠ Q 5
♡ A K Q 7 3
♢ 6
♣ A 10 8 5 4

♠ A J 10 6
♡ J 10 4 2
♢ 8 4
♣ Q 7 3

♠ 8 4
♡ 9 5
♢ K Q J 3
♣ K J 9 6 2

♠ K 9 7 3 2
♡ 8 6
♢ A 10 9 7 5 2
♣ —

Game all
Dealer South

South	West	North	East
Pass	Pass	1♡	Pass
1♠	Pass	2♣	Pass
2♢	Pass	3♣	Pass
3♢	Pass	3♠	Pass
4♠	Pass	Pass	Pass

The ace and another spade would have been the best start for the defence, but Hamman led the two of hearts to dummy's queen. The declarer ruffed a club in hand, cashed the diamond ace and ruffed a diamond, cashed the aces of hearts and clubs, ruffed another club and played the seven of diamonds in the diagram position.

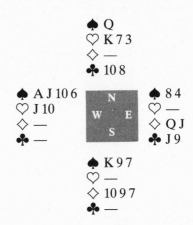

♠ Q
♡ K 7 3
♢ —
♣ 10 8

♠ A J 10 6   ♠ 8 4
♡ J 10   ♡ —
♢ —   ♢ Q J
♣ —   ♣ J 9

♠ K 9 7
♡ —
♢ 10 9 7
♣ —

Hamman had a wide choice of actions at this point. He realised that it would not do to ruff with the ace of spades and return a trump. Declarer would then ruff a heart and score his tenth trick with the king of spades. Nor would it help to throw a heart on the diamond. After ruffing with the queen of spades, South would ruff a heart and play another diamond. West, with nothing but trumps left, would have to ruff and concede a tenth trick to the king of spades.

So Hamman decided to ruff the seven of diamonds with the six of spades. Declarer over-ruffed in dummy and could have made his contract by ruffing a low heart and then exiting with a trump. West, after drawing trumps, would have to concede the last trick to the king of hearts.

However, the declarer failed to recognise the need to keep a winner in dummy. After scoring the queen of spades, he continued with the king of hearts from the table. This was ruffed and over-ruffed, and on the diamond continuation West was able to throw his winning heart. East won this trick and West took the rest.

Hamman's defence was very good, but it fell just short of perfection. After a heart lead the declarer can always succeed on the actual lie of the cards, but the eight and the nine of spades might have been interchanged as shown in the new diagram.

Now, for the defence to prevail against anything declarer may try, West has to ruff the seven of diamonds with the jack or the ten of spades!

♠ Q
♡ K 7 3
◇ —
♣ 10 8

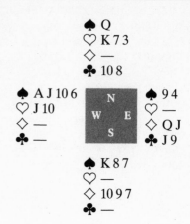

♠ A J 10 6   ♠ 9 4
♡ J 10   ♡ —
◇ —   ◇ Q J
♣ —   ♣ J 9

♠ K 8 7
♡ —
◇ 10 9 7
♣ —

A fascinating problem in pairs technique was posed by this hand from a Polish tournament.

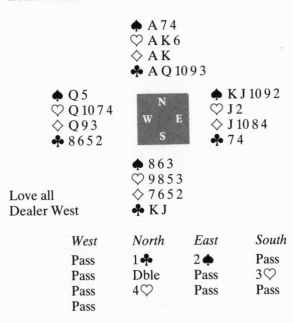

```
                    ♠ A 7 4
                    ♡ A K 6
                    ◇ A K
                    ♣ A Q 10 9 3
     ♠ Q 5                          ♠ K J 10 9 2
     ♡ Q 10 7 4        N            ♡ J 2
     ◇ Q 9 3       W       E        ◇ J 10 8 4
     ♣ 8 6 5 2        S             ♣ 7 4
                    ♠ 8 6 3
                    ♡ 9 8 5 3
Love all            ◇ 7 6 5 2
Dealer West         ♣ K J
```

West	North	East	South
Pass	1♣	2♠	Pass
Pass	Dble	Pass	3♡
Pass	4♡	Pass	Pass
Pass			

It was a dull hand at many tables in the tournament. The normal contract was three no-trumps and the declarers made the obvious ten tricks. But at a few tables, after a strong club from North and a weak jump overcall from East, South became declarer in a precarious contract of four hearts.

Winning the opening lead of the queen of spades with dummy's ace, the declarers drew two rounds of trumps with the ace and king and then set about the clubs, discarding spades from hand. All went well when West had to follow to four rounds, leaving the position shown in the diagram.

What should South do now? It is easy enough to establish a tenth trick by playing the fifth club and discarding a diamond from hand, but the declarers who adopted this course were disappointed with the outcome. Plus 420 brought in few match-points since the norm was plus 430.

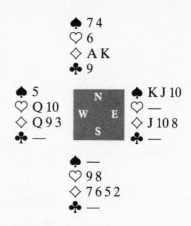

♠ 7 4
♡ 6
◇ A K
♣ 9

♠ 5
♡ Q 10
◇ Q 9 3
♣ —

♠ K J 10
♡ —
◇ J 10 8
♣ —

♠ —
♡ 9 8
◇ 7 6 5 2
♣ —

Declarer needs to score eleven tricks in hearts to beat the field, and this will be possible only if West has a second spade in spite of the evidence of the bidding. South must ruff a spade in the diagram position, and when West follows suit the rest is plain sailing. South crosses to dummy with a diamond and ruffs the third spade. West over-ruffs and draws the last trump, but the declarer scores the last two tricks in dummy with the diamond winner and the long club.

Declarer can also come to eleven tricks, in more hair-raising fashion, by ruffing a diamond in dummy before running the clubs.

In the pairs game making the contract does not always ensure a good score. It may be necessary to make an overtrick in order to pull in a respectable quota of match-points. Sometimes the overtrick will arrive gift-wrapped through a friendly opening lead. More often, as in the following hand, it has to be earned.

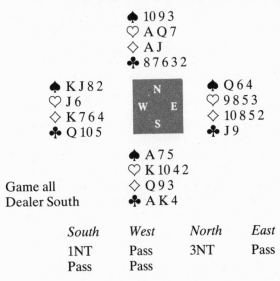

```
                    ♠ 10 9 3
                    ♡ A Q 7
                    ◇ A J
                    ♣ 8 7 6 3 2
    ♠ K J 8 2                        ♠ Q 6 4
    ♡ J 6              N             ♡ 9 8 5 3
    ◇ K 7 6 4      W       E         ◇ 10 8 5 2
    ♣ Q 10 5           S             ♣ J 9
                    ♠ A 7 5
                    ♡ K 10 4 2
Game all            ◇ Q 9 3
Dealer South        ♣ A K 4
```

South	*West*	*North*	*East*
1NT	Pass	3NT	Pass
Pass	Pass		

At most tables West found the best lead of the two of spades, and South naturally held up his ace until the third round. A number of declarers continued with three rounds of clubs, hoping that East would have to win. West produced the queen of clubs on the third round, however, and promptly cashed the last spade to hold the contract to nine tricks.

At one table South realised that he had nothing to lose by playing a couple of rounds of hearts before testing the clubs. The fall of the heart jack from West made nine tricks secure, and it became clear that West must have the club stopper. For if West had started with more than four diamonds he would surely have led that suit in preference to spades.

123

South therefore continued with two more rounds of hearts, forcing West to weaken his hand in one way or another. This was the position when the last heart was led:

On the play of the heart ten West could not throw a club without allowing South to make eleven tricks. If he parted with his winning spade, South would discard the jack of diamonds from dummy and continue with three rounds of clubs to establish a tenth trick.

In practice West discarded another diamond, but this did not help him. South threw a club from dummy, finessed the jack of diamonds and cashed the ace, then returned to hand with a club to score the queen of diamonds as his tenth trick.

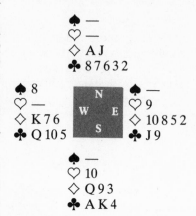

Technically West was subjected to a three-suit strip-squeeze, but you do not need to know the jargon in order to execute such a squeeze. Just play your cards in a sensible order and you will usually be able to tell when an opponent is in trouble.

52   *Table Presents*

Bridge is a game of mistakes, and many of those mistakes seem to be made when defending against three no-trumps. Look at this example from a match between Sweden and Finland in the Nordic Championships.

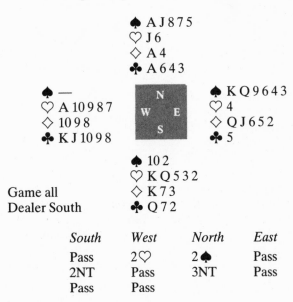

```
              ♠ A J 8 7 5
              ♡ J 6
              ◇ A 4
              ♣ A 6 4 3
♠ —                             ♠ K Q 9 6 4 3
♡ A 10 9 8 7      N             ♡ 4
◇ 10 9 8     W        E         ◇ Q J 6 5 2
♣ K J 10 9 8      S             ♣ 5
              ♠ 10 2
              ♡ K Q 5 3 2
Game all      ◇ K 7 3
Dealer South  ♣ Q 7 2
```

South	West	North	East
Pass	2♡	2♠	Pass
2NT	Pass	3NT	Pass
Pass	Pass		

The bid of two hearts showed 5-5 in either hearts and clubs or spades and diamonds, and it soon became abundantly clear which two suits West held.

The lead of the ten of hearts went to dummy's jack and the declarer, Magnus Lindqvist of Sweden, continued with the five of spades from the table. East contributed the three and South, expecting a singleton honour on his left, put in the two. Greatly to his surprise the five of spades held the trick, West discarding the eight of diamonds. That made two mistakes on the same trick! If East had played a spade honour and had switched to a diamond, the contract would have had no chance. And South

125

would still have been doomed if West had discarded a club. In throwing a diamond West deprived himself of a vital exit card.

With a perfect count of the hand, Lindqvist was quick to seize his opportunity. He cashed the king and ace of diamonds and then played a second heart to the queen and ace. West returned a heart to the king but was immediately put back on lead to cash his remaining hearts. With nothing but clubs left in his hand, West tried a lead of the king which was allowed to win a fourth trick for the defence. This was the position:

The next club was won in dummy with the ace. East was able to discard a diamond on this trick, but he was squeezed in spades and diamonds when South continued with a club to his queen.

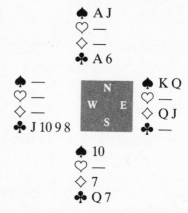

Did you spot West's final mistake? That spectacular play of the club king was not the right move on this occasion. If West had played the jack of clubs instead of the king declarer might have ducked in both hands, but the continuation of another low club would have been a killer. South has to win with the queen, and East escapes the pressure because the squeeze card—the ace of clubs—is in the wrong hand.

Borderline game contracts on a 4-4 trump fit can be tricky to play and hard to defend against. Here is a four-spade hand from a Swiss teams.

```
                    ♠ K Q 6 4
                    ♡ J 9
                    ♢ A Q 3
                    ♣ K 7 6 3
      ♠ 7 3                           ♠ A 10 9
      ♡ Q 10 8 2                      ♡ 6 5
      ♢ K 8                           ♢ J 10 9 5 4 2
      ♣ A Q 10 8 4                    ♣ 9 5
                    ♠ J 8 5 2
                    ♡ A K 7 4 3
N–S game            ♢ 7 6
Dealer North        ♣ J 2
```

West	North	East	South
	1NT	Pass	2♢*
Pass	2♡	Pass	2♠**
Pass	3♠	Pass	4♠
Pass	Pass	Pass	

*transfer to hearts   ** 4-card suit*

Seeking to protect his heart holding, West chose to lead a trump. East captured dummy's king with the ace and returned the ten of spades to the queen. The declarer cashed the ace and king of hearts and continued with a third heart which was ruffed in dummy and over-ruffed by East. The remaining cards are shown in the diagram.

South was known to
have four cards in the
minor suits, and there
could be no hope for the
defence if these cards
included a high honour.
East decided to return
the nine of clubs, but
this was not good
enough. The nine ran to
dummy's king and a
second club was won by
West. South ruffed the
third club in hand, ruf-
fed a heart in dummy

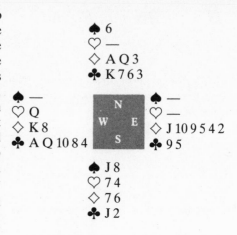

♠ 6
♡ —
◇ A Q 3
♣ K 7 6 3

♠ —
♡ Q
◇ K 8
♣ A Q 10 8 4

♠ —
♡ —
◇ J 10 9 5 4 2
♣ 9 5

♠ J 8
♡ 7 4
◇ 7 6
♣ J 2

and returned to hand with another club ruff. After cashing the
established heart he was able to finesse in diamonds for ten
tricks.

It was difficult for East to choose between dummy's tenaces,
but close analysis shows that a diamond is the right return no
matter how South's cards in the minors are distributed. Why
should a diamond be more effective than a club? The basic
reason is that declarer is denied a second entry to his hand. On
winning the diamond return he can cash the second diamond
winner and ruff the third diamond, but he has no good continuation. If he plays on clubs he is unable to set up his long heart, and
if he sets up the heart he has to play clubs from the table.

Declarer could have succeeded by drawing the third trump at
trick three, finessing the queen of diamonds and ducking a heart,
but this sequence of plays is far from obvious.

At the 1988 Olympiad the Polish team disappointed its supporters by failing to reach the quarter finals, but the players had the consolation of a 21-9 win in the round robin against the eventual winners, the USA. The margin would have been greater if the Poles had been firing on all cylinders on this hand.

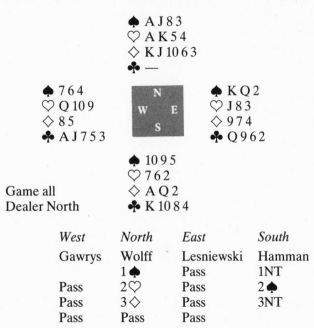

```
              ♠ A J 8 3
              ♡ A K 5 4
              ◇ K J 10 6 3
              ♣ —
  ♠ 7 6 4            N            ♠ K Q 2
  ♡ Q 10 9      W        E        ♡ J 8 3
  ◇ 8 5            S            ◇ 9 7 4
  ♣ A J 7 5 3                    ♣ Q 9 6 2
              ♠ 10 9 5
              ♡ 7 6 2
Game all      ◇ A Q 2
Dealer North  ♣ K 10 8 4
```

West	North	East	South
Gawrys	Wolff	Lesniewski	Hamman
	1♠	Pass	1NT
Pass	2♡	Pass	2♠
Pass	3◇	Pass	3NT
Pass	Pass	Pass	

After an Orange Club sequence Hamman finished in three no-trumps. As you can see, he has eight top tricks and the natural lead of a club would provide the ninth. Suspecting as much, Gawrys found the only way to give the defence a chance when he led the ten of hearts.

An immediate duck would have established a ninth trick but this was not obvious at the table. Rather than rely entirely on the heart split, Hamman won the trick with the heart ace, came to hand with the ace of diamonds and ran the ten of spades to East's king. Perhaps expecting his partner to have started with four hearts, Lesniewski returned the jack of hearts which was ducked all round. Next came a low club to the eight and jack, dummy discarding a spade. West switched back to a spade and Hamman was at the crossroads. Eventually he did the right thing by rising with the ace of spades and playing for the heart split.

East missed a great opportunity when in with the king of spades at trick three. Just look at what happens if he returns a club immediately. Dummy is squeezed and declarer has to abandon one of his major-suit options. If a heart is discarded, the threat of the long heart disappears and West can switch back to hearts. Similarly, if dummy gives up a spade it is safe for West to switch back to spades. Whatever happens the defenders must make five tricks.

Four spades looks a hazardous contract on this hand from the 1988 Olympiad in Venice, but many of the declarers in the round robin managed to find a way home. Here is the action in the match between Denmark and Finland.

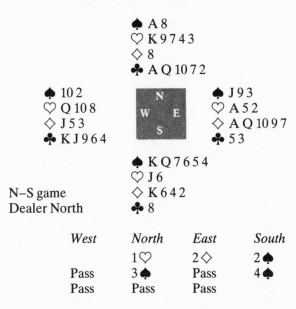

```
                ♠ A 8
                ♡ K 9 7 4 3
                ◇ 8
                ♣ A Q 10 7 2
  ♠ 10 2                           ♠ J 9 3
  ♡ Q 10 8                         ♡ A 5 2
  ◇ J 5 3                          ◇ A Q 10 9 7
  ♣ K J 9 6 4                      ♣ 5 3
                ♠ K Q 7 6 5 4
                ♡ J 6
N–S game        ◇ K 6 4 2
Dealer North    ♣ 8
```

	West	North	East	South
		1♡	2◇	2♠
	Pass	3♣	Pass	4♠
	Pass	Pass	Pass	

For Denmark, Stig Werdelin played in four spades after the above sequence. West led the three of diamonds to his partner's ace and East switched to a trump, won by dummy's ace. Declarer saw that he could organise a diamond ruff or a club finesse but not both. Since the club finesse was not sure to succeed, he cashed the ace of clubs, ruffed a club in hand, ruffed a diamond on the table and ruffed another club. When the outstanding trumps had been drawn the position was as shown in the diagram.

Declarer led the seven of spades, discarding a heart from dummy, and East was caught in a strip-squeeze. If he discarded a diamond, he would be end-played in diamonds and forced to yield a trick to the king of hearts. In practice East threw a heart, and declarer simply ducked a heart to set up his ninth trick. If Werdelin had discarded a club instead of a heart on the last spade and if East had still bared the heart ace, a surprise

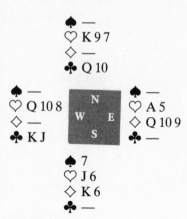

overtrick would have been made when West was squeezed on the forced diamond return.

In the other room the Finns bid to four spades without interference and Willy Dam found the good lead of a trump. The declarer won in dummy and played a low heart towards his jack. On a different lie of the cards this might have been the winning play. As it was, West won with the queen and switched to a club to remove the heart threat. East played a second trump when in with the ace of diamonds and the declarer had to be satisfied with nine tricks.

Can four spades be made on the lead of the two of spades? It is not easy to read the position of the cards in the absence of enemy bidding, but declarer can succeed if he plays the diamond from dummy at trick two. East will no doubt take his ace and return a trump, and declarer applies a spot of pressure with three more rounds of trumps. West cannot afford to discard more than one heart, and if he throws a diamond declarer can achieve an ending similar to that reached by Werdelin. West may well discard one heart and two clubs to produce this ending:

Declarer finesses in clubs, discards a diamond on the club ace and continues with a club ruff to put the question to East. As before, a heart discard allows the overtrick, and a diamond discard is countered by king and another diamond. Even if East unblocks to let

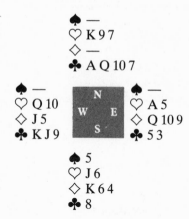

West win the trick, a correct guess on the heart return brings success for declarer.

There is another possible scenario. Suppose East plays low at trick two, allowing the king of diamonds to win. Declarer has to proceed with care. He cannot afford to take his diamond ruff immediately since there is no convenient way back to hand. He must play on clubs first, finessing the club queen, discarding a diamond on the ace and continuing with a third club. East does best to ruff with the nine of spades, forcing declarer to over-ruff. A diamond is ruffed in dummy and a fourth club is played. East again makes a nuisance of himself by ruffing with the spade jack, but declarer counters by discarding his last diamond. He ruffs the diamond return low and draws the oustanding trump to finish with ten tricks, losing just one trump and two hearts.

Borderline game contracts are notoriously difficult to defend against since there are so many ways for the defenders to go wrong. Here is an example from a team event.

```
                    ♠ A 10 3
                    ♡ A 8 7 2
                    ◇ A 8 4
                    ♣ A K Q

    ♠ K 7                          ♠ Q 8 2
    ♡ 10 6 5 4          N          ♡ K Q J 9 3
    ◇ 5            W        E       ◇ K Q J 7
    ♣ 9 8 7 5 3 2      S            ♣ 6

                    ♠ J 9 6 5 4
                    ♡ —
Love all            ◇ 10 9 6 3 2
Dealer East         ♣ J 10 4
```

West	North	East	South
		1♡	Pass
2♡	Dble	3♡	Pass
Pass	Dble	Pass	4♠
Pass	Pass	Pass	

After holding his peace for a couple of rounds, South woke up and decided to make an interesting game of it.

West led the five of diamonds, the four was played from dummy and East won the trick with the jack. The king of diamonds was returned and West ruffed with the seven of spades. This was hardly a dynamic defence. The declarer won the club switch and cashed the ace of spades, felling the king. The ace of diamonds was unblocked, and a heart ruff in hand was followed by a diamond ruff in dummy. When the ten of spades was played from the table East scored the third and last defensive trick with the queen of spades.

East pointed out that the contract could have been defeated if West had not wasted a trump on the king of diamonds. This is true enough, but the defenders still have to exercise a little care. If West discards a heart on the king of diamonds, declarer wins with the ace, ruffs a heart in hand and runs the nine of spades to East's queen. But now East can let his partner ruff the low diamond, and a club switch from West makes declarer's task too difficult.

A superficial analysis at the time suggested that an original heart lead would also defeat the contract. Not so. Declarer can ruff the heart in hand and run the nine of spades to the queen. East may return a club, but declarer wins, ruffs another heart, plays a spade to the king and ace and ruffs a third heart in hand. A diamond to the ace puts dummy in to draw the last trump, and the defenders are limited to one trump trick and two diamonds.

Ah, but suppose that West covers the nine of spades with the king at trick two. A nice try but no coconut, for this does not seriously impede the dummy reversal. Declarer wins with the ace, ruffs another heart, plays a club to the queen and ruffs a third heart to reach this position:

The play of the jack of spades again leaves the defenders with no more than three tricks.

Surely there must be other ways of defeating this ambitious game. Indeed there are.

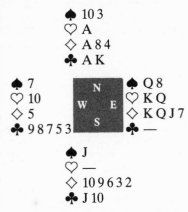

```
            ♠ 10 3
            ♡ A
            ◇ A 8 4
            ♣ A K
♠ 7                      ♠ Q 8
♡ 10        N            ♡ K Q
◇ 5      W     E         ◇ K Q J 7
♣ 9 8 7 5 3   S          ♣ —
            ♠ J
            ♡ —
            ◇ 10 9 6 3 2
            ♣ J 10
```

If West starts with a club he takes out one of declarer's entries prematurely and the dummy reversal becomes impossible to handle. South may ruff a heart in hand and play the nine of spades, but West can cover to force out the ace. A second heart ruff is followed by a diamond to the ace and a third heart ruff to leave the position shown in the diagram, but when East comes in with the queen of spades he can force dummy with the third round of diamonds to secure a second trump trick for the defence.

```
            ♠ 10 3
            ♡ A
            ◇ 8 4
            ♣ A K
♠ 7                      ♠ Q 8
♡ 10         N           ♡ K Q
◇ —       W     E        ◇ K Q J
♣ 8 7 5 3 2    S         ♣ —
            ♠ J
            ♡ —
            ◇ 10 9 6 3
            ♣ J 10
```

And then there is always the possibility of an initial trump lead. Many defenders would hesitate to lead a trump from a holding such as king and another, but if West starts with either the king or the seven of spades the declarer has no chance of making his contract.

On the actual defence it is worth noting that East was not entirely blameless. If he had switched to either a club or a trump at trick two, his partner would have had no problems.

57 *Troubled Waters*

This hand from a recent tournament in Switzerland features a sparkling defence by a young oriental player, Duong Hong, who is now resident in Lausanne. The deal was originally reported by Jean Besse in the *Journal de Genève*.

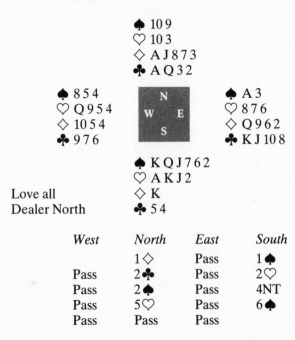

```
                    ♠ 10 9
                    ♡ 10 3
                    ◇ A J 8 7 3
                    ♣ A Q 3 2
  ♠ 8 5 4                          ♠ A 3
  ♡ Q 9 5 4         N              ♡ 8 7 6
  ◇ 10 5 4       W     E           ◇ Q 9 6 2
  ♣ 9 7 6           S              ♣ K J 10 8
                    ♠ K Q J 7 6 2
                    ♡ A K J 2
Love all             ◇ K
Dealer North         ♣ 5 4
```

West	North	East	South
	1◇	Pass	1♠
Pass	2♣	Pass	2♡
Pass	2♠	Pass	4NT
Pass	5♡	Pass	6♠
Pass	Pass	Pass	

West led the six of clubs against the spade slam. Not tempted to risk everything on an immediate finesse, South went up with the ace of clubs. After a diamond to the king, he played off the top hearts, ruffed his small heart on the table and discarded his club loser on the ace of diamonds. A club ruff left the position shown in the diagram.

South continued with the jack of hearts and ruffed in dummy with the ten of spades. Consider East's options at this point. If he discards a diamond, South can ruff a diamond and play the king of spades: if he discards a club, South will ruff a club and play the king of spades. In either case the defenders are restricted to one trick.

Without hesitation, Duong Hong in the East seat threw the three of spades under dummy's ten. This under-ruffing coup kept alive the chance of promoting a trump in his partner's hand.

```
              ♠ 10
              ♡ —
              ◇ J 8 3
              ♣ Q 3
  ♠ 8 5 4              ♠ A 3
  ♡ Q        N         ♡ —
  ◇ 10     W   E       ◇ Q 9
  ♣ 9        S         ♣ K J
              ♠ K Q J 7 6
              ♡ J
              ◇ —
              ♣ —
```

South returned to hand with a club ruff and led the king of spades. Now, on winning with the ace, East was able to play his fourth club and promote the setting trick for his partner.

What happened when South ruffed the fourth heart in dummy was that East was caught in a non-material backwash squeeze. He could throw a club on a diamond without material loss, but he would give up all chance of a trump promotion in the suit of his discard. The discard of the small trump is, of course, equally fatal if declarer reads the position correctly. After ruffing himself back to hand South can lead his remaining small trump to knock out the ace.

But such endings are hard to read with any certainty. For all South knew, the full hand could be as follows:

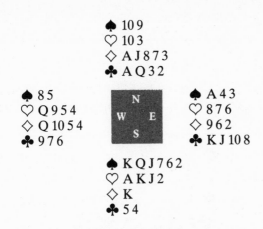

♠ 10 9
♡ 10 3
◇ A J 8 7 3
♣ A Q 3 2

♠ 8 5
♡ Q 9 5 4
◇ Q 10 5 4
♣ 9 7 6

♠ A 4 3
♡ 8 7 6
◇ 9 6 2
♣ K J 10 8

♠ K Q J 7 6 2
♡ A K J 2
◇ K
♣ 5 4

Now East might bring off a fabulous coup by under-ruffing on the fourth round of hearts. If South exits with his low trump after returning to hand with a ruff, he goes down in a stone-cold contract.

Here is a hand for those who appreciate fine technique. It was played by Scottish international Jack Paterson in a pairs tournament in Brittany.

```
                    ♠ 10 3
                    ♡ K Q 7 5
                    ◇ Q 10 7 4 3
                    ♣ A K

 ♠ A Q 5                          ♠ J 8 7 4 2
 ♡ 10 9            N              ♡ 3
 ◇ 9 5 2        W     E           ◇ A K J 8 6
 ♣ J 10 9 6 4      S              ♣ 7 3

                    ♠ K 9 6
                    ♡ A J 8 6 4 2
 Game all           ◇ —
 Dealer North       ♣ Q 8 5 2
```

West	North	East	South
	1◇	Pass	1♡
Pass	3♡	Pass	3♠
Pass	4♣	Pass	4◇
Pass	5♣	Pass	6♡
Pass	Pass	Pass	

Against this ambitious slam West led the ten of hearts and the trick was won in dummy with the queen. When a low diamond was played East went in with the jack. South ruffed, returned to dummy with the king of clubs and continued with the ten of diamonds which was covered by the king and ruffed.

From the play to the first few tricks it seemed clear that East had started with all the diamond honours. It was therefore unlikely that the spade ace would be favourably placed. Paterson decided to continue on cross-ruff lines and hope for something to turn up. He played a club to the ace, ruffed a third diamond and cashed the queen of clubs, discarding the three of spades from the table. When East also discarded a spade there was a glimmer of light at the end of the tunnel. South ruffed his fourth club in dummy and returned the ten of spades in the position shown in the diagram.

If East covers the ten of spades South plays low. West cannot afford to overtake, and the rest of the tricks are made on a complete cross-ruff.

In practice East played low on the spade lead and West won with the queen, but the defenders were still in poor shape. West had to return his trump to prevent the cross-ruff, but when the king of

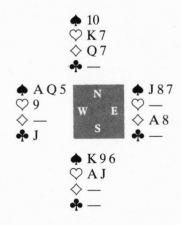

♠ 10
♡ K 7
♢ Q 7
♣ —

♠ A Q 5   ♠ J 8 7
♡ 9   ♡ —
♢ —   ♢ A 8
♣ J   ♣ —

♠ K 9 6
♡ A J
♢ —
♣ —

hearts was played from dummy East was caught in an overtaking trump squeeze. If he discarded a diamond, declarer would play low from his hand and ruff a diamond to establish his twelfth trick. When East chose the alternative discard of a spade, South overtook the king of hearts with his ace and played the king of spades, ruffing out the ace and pinning the jack to set up his twelfth trick in spades.

It's an ending to delight the heart of the connoisseur.